STAYING SANE

A STRUGGLE OF SURVIVAL

BY

EMMA VOLESKY

TABLE OF CONTENTS

STAYING SANE: A STRUGGLE OF SURVIVAL............................1

PART - 1 4

PART - 2 42

PART - 3 65

PART - 4 181

PART - 5 218

PART - 6 236

STAYING SANE:
A STRUGGLE OF SURVIVAL

—————○—————

Emma Volesky was seventeen years old when she first began advocating for people who live with serious mental illness. Emma had been diagnosed with Bipolar Disorder at eight years old and endured multiple hospitalizations.

As part of advocacy training, Emma wrote down her story of what it was like to be overwhelmed by mental illness and accompanying hallucinations at such a young age. I read the first two pages of her amazing story and told her that she needed to write a book to spread her message of hope to other young people and their families.

This is that book. It is as powerful as I knew it would be. An amazing view of what it is like to be struck by mental illness and then fight for recovery."

Matt Kuntz, J.D.

Executive Director, NAMI Montana

"Putting all the emotions together isn't the hardest part. The hardest part is trying to figure out those emotions. Your mind falters for excuses even though the answer is right in front of you. You try to get a hold of it at once. The more you try, the more you fail. The less you try, the more you fail. You fail every single time. There are a million different feelings, and you're not even sure what you want. Do you want to be honest or dishonest? Do you want to be happy or sad? Do you want to be alive or dead? What is real and what is not real? All the unknown feelings overwhelm you until you can't do anything about it, except go deeper and deeper into your own misery. Soon you are in a bottomless pit and there is nothing you can do, and you can't escape. This is one description of my life. I can tell it in a lighter or heavier text. The situation is the same: a life of never-ending pain."

Emma Volesky

To my parents Doug and Joannie
&
My six siblings Megan, Danny, Ellie, Paul, Jack, and Nick
Thanks for saving me a million times.
I love you all!!!

Note to Readers:

Staying Sane: A Struggle of Survival is a memoir I poured my whole heart and soul into. It portrays how serious a severe mental illness is. A few people have told me that it's a negative story. That is not my intention at all. Yes, my memoir has some very dark and very powerful parts, but it is an honest and sometimes brutal portrayal of just how serious mental illness is. Mental illness is real. It's happening right now. What I'm writing isn't intended to be negative. It's intended to show the honest truth. I am writing the truth. The truth is real, and guess what? It is harsh but it's also full of hope. Hope... It's what pulled me through. I hope that when you read this book you'll keep in mind that recovery IS possible. It happens. I promise. XOXOXOXOXO! - Emma

PART - 1

Identifying Data:

This is a 15-year-old who resides with her parents in Helena. She was referred for admission by Dr. --- and was first evaluated and medically cleared at St. Peter's Emergency Department in Helena, Montana.

The pain is unbearable. When I say unbearable, I mean there is no escape. It's like hell. I won't be surprised if hell is like this. I won't be surprised if I am even in hell or if the pain I feel is even worse than hell. The pain feels physical, emotional, and mental all at once. It's so powerful and strong that if it was possible to escape, I would do anything to myself. When I say anything…. I mean anything. I will cry harder than ever, no matter how tiring it is. I will slice my wrists a thousand times. I will swear to myself to say that "I'm worthless" nonstop in a way that doesn't have any trace of value whatsoever. I will even kill myself….

This brings me back to the present. Why I am here today at this unknown hospital. My eyes flicker to my parents, who are smiling at me as we follow a lady into the hospital in Missoula. My feet move as if this is normal. I am fully aware that my mind is in the wrong state because I am so unsure, yet so sure at the same time. We go into an elevator and I watch the doors close, sealing me from the outside world. When the elevator opens, the lady takes out her ID card and puts it to the identification square on the side of the wall. It opens, and we walk through the door. I don't need to look back to see that it's yet another door that will seal me out from the outside world. My feet keep moving as we go past more doors that are locked from the inside and the outside. We finally come to the last door. I slowly cross the threshold. I take in the scene around me. There are adults in scrubs to my left and in front of me is a desk with video monitors of rooms behind it. It's hard to tear my gaze away from the monitors. I know exactly what they are for. They are put in everyone's room to watch them 24/7. There is no privacy for anything. Not to change, not to sleep, not even to try to kill oneself. They are to keep us safe. I know that's the main purpose. I just suddenly wish that I could have some privacy. Can't a 15-year-old have that much? The lady takes us to the right, which I soon figure out isn't for adults, but for teenagers like me. At least I don't have to be with adults. Still, I know that whatever happens, the pain won't ever go away.

I sit next to my dad as my mom grabs a clipboard with a pen connected to it. It's paperwork again, just like they did in the ER at St. Peter's Hospital back at home in Helena where I was evaluated. My mind drifts back to the hours of waiting at the ER. We saw a lady clutching her husband's leg with one hand because her other hand was bleeding hard through a tablecloth. There was an older man to one side of the couch in a wheelchair talking so rapidly that I couldn't make sense of what his words even were. My dad was doing the paperwork. It just took minutes to get in, but it didn't feel that way. Hopefully it won't take as long here. I don't know why I hope that though, because my parents have to head back home tomorrow after a short meeting with a doctor in the morning. Back home is where everyone is. My dad gently pulls me into a hug as I lean into his shoulder. I look up at the ceiling when my mom comes back with the lady. I can't tell what my parents are thinking. For once I don't have to worry about what I might be doing wrong because there's nothing more left to be done wrong.

I stand up as the lady takes me to a room where I can clearly see where the camera can see me. There's two beds and they are both empty. My dad sets my bag of clothes on a desk against the wall. The curtains are drawn, and I know the sky is as dark as ever. My eyes glance to a door which must be the bathroom. I don't need to use the toilet or anything, but I'm hoping it isn't like my first hospitalization five years ago, where the bathrooms were locked. I must confirm this, so I walk over and hold my breath as I turn the knob. It isn't locked. I open it and look inside. It's a normal bathroom. I'm about to shut the door when I see that there's no lock on the inside of it. This doesn't bother me. It might not be as bad as before. I try not to doubt this. My parents hold out their arms for a hug. I take each of their hugs hard and try not to cry. I know they will be back tomorrow, but I don't know for how long. When my parents leave there is something in me that breaks. I crawl into bed in the clothes I wore all day and go under the covers of this unknown bed. I curl into a ball and cry myself to sleep with the unbearable pain eating me up inside.

Identifying Data:

[The patient] describes frequent suicidal thoughts and thinks about how much better off she would be in heaven and not dealing with her current pain, secondary to her psychiatric illness. She has felt this way for the past two days, and it was much worse yesterday. She feels much better so far today. She was not sure if she could stay safe at home. She cannot recall past suicide attempts. She does remember cutting her wrist Sunday and does not know why; she rarely cuts. She denies homicidal ideation. In April she had images of mutilating her family, but this was apparently secondary to hearing a story about someone being mutilated. She denies any intent or actual thoughts about harming her family.

The next morning, I am numb. I am number than numb. I heave in a deep breath when a different lady than last night comes into the bedroom. She smiles, but I don't have the energy or desire to smile back. She leads me out the door to another little room where my parents are. Hope rises within me that I might be able to go home, but when I see a doctor and a lady with a clipboard there, the hope shatters into a million pieces. I imagine me taking those pieces and stabbing them as deep as they can go into my chest. There I go again, thinking about killing myself. I force this longing out of my mind and sit down in a chair right between my parents. The doctor has gray hair with glasses. The lady with the clipboard has long blonde hair. I say the first words I really have ever said since what happened back at home. "I'm just wondering how long I have to stay here…." The doctor smiles softly. The smile is a little too soft for me. I shift, uncomfortable in my seat. I immediately regret this because I know they are watching my every move. I have to pretend that I'm fine.

"At least a week, Emma," he says. I shift again and curse at myself silently. He knows my name. Does that mean he knows everything that has happened? "I'm Dr. Fleed," he says.

I nod a slow nod. I regret this too. I feel like I have to act as normal as possible. My every move has to be careful. I just hate that this makes it even harder to be here.

The lady with the clipboard sets it down beside her. It's her turn to introduce herself.

"I'm Ashley."

I don't have anything to say back because I'm so confused if saying something will mean I have to stay or if saying something means I have to go. I nod again to show that I'm thinking this. This paranoia is another thing I hate. There are so many levels of paranoia and that makes me so fearful. I know this pretty well. Just ask anyone who knows me well and they will agree quicker than the speed of light.

"Emma, can you tell us why you're here?" Dr. Fleed asks.

My throat closes up and I almost choke. I hate this so much. He obviously knows I'm here, so why ask me? Doesn't he get that this is so painful? He is really going to make me say what I'm thinking. What will it be like to talk about it and not think it? Dr. Fleed and Ashley wait patiently. I dare a quick look at my parents. Their lips are spread into smiles, but the smiles are half real and it's probably just as possible that they are hurting at least half as much as I am. I begin to hate Dr. Fleed. I almost wish he could be in my place, wanting to kill himself, but I don't. No one deserves this. I now begin to hate myself for almost wishing this upon a man who is most likely only trying help me. I don't think it's possible to hate myself any more than I do now though.

I open my mouth and almost begin to speak the words. I stop myself before the words I was trying to cut myself to death come out of my mouth. I don't want to go into details. I rethink how to put this into words. It might seem simple, but it takes a lot of thought in a short period of time to say what I say next. "I was suicidal."

I see right away that Ashley writes this on a piece of notebook paper that's on the clipboard. I set my jaw. Of course, they're going to record this. I suppose it's required to keep track. Keeping track upsets me so much. Dr. Fleed waits for me to go on.

"I, um, was suicidal so much that it hurt." Dr. Fleed's eyes grow even softer. It looks like this is going nowhere. I decide to tell the truth in deeper context to get this over with. Well, sort of a deeper context, that is. "I was cutting myself with a knife because I was so depressed. I could only focus on that because the pain was too much for me to handle."

My voice cracks with emotion on the word *pain*. I stop and look up into Dr. Fleed's eyes. Seeing them the softest yet makes me want to get all that happened out of my mouth. The sooner the better, I suppose. I think back. Tears blur my vision and I close my eyes to force them back in. If I cry, this will show them how weak I am. That is a thing I usually want. I want people to see how weak I am because they will get a sense of what I'm feeling, but I need to be strong here. I need to be super strong, so I can get out of here. I open my eyes, but tears are now flowing down my cheeks. I dare another look at my parents, but this time it's not in my control. I have to see if they're crying too. They almost are and the only reason they aren't is because they are struggling to keep it in. They are trying to be tough for me.

Checking to see if my parents cry has always been something I wanted to check even before I was sick like this. If it was in church after a sad story or after watching a very poignant movie or even if it was a funeral, I was always fascinated by it. Now, seeing those holding in their tears makes me ache.

"Well we're here to help you get better," Dr. Fleed reassures me.

It's nothing near reassuring. It's more of a dreadful promise. I try to smile but I can't.

"Emma, you need to tell me more about you being suicidal."

I take in a deep breath. "I guess being suicidal made me want to kill myself." This is a stupid and obvious response. I back pedal my words as much as I can. I just hope that it isn't too late to take back those words which make me sound so idiotic. I soon make the choice to be honest. The want to leave this room is too powerful. "I was suicidal for a reason that's not really explainable. I just hurt so much with all the emotions going on. I don't know if I was even going to kill myself exactly, so I started out cutting my wrist. I couldn't really go further because I was so paranoid that my family would come home soon. By the time they did, I was so shaken up that I couldn't even think about killing myself that much."

The tears are uncontrollable by now. I'm shaking so hard and oh God here is the weak me. So much for needing to be strong. I can't even bring myself to see if Ashley is sympathetic enough to stop recording on paper even for a moment.

Dr. Fleed motions to the lady who brought me to this little room. I see that she is wearing scrubs. To my horror I realize I'm going to have to wear scrubs too. I stand up and follow her out of the room, not daring another look at my parents because I fear I'll break down. That's the last thing I need is to break down and to get another soft look from Dr. Fleed. When I reach my bedroom, the lady speaks to me nicely.

"I'm going to be your nurse for today. You can call me Sarah."

11

"I'm Emma."

"It's nice to meet you," she says.

I want to respond with something like, *it's too bad I don't feel the same way.* I don't though, because it'll get me nowhere. She takes something out of the bag I just now notice she's carrying. My jaw drops open as I see the same colored scrubs as hers. She seems oblivious to my reaction. I shut my jaw quickly.

"You're going to have to put this on, hon."

Really, I do my best not to make my worst grimace. She gives the scrubs to me. I'm about to put them on when she tells me something that makes me want to put on my worst grimace.

"You can't wear a bra because of safety issues." She walks out of the room and I start to cry a little. She is actually serious. This is a new type of torture. I want to scream at the top of my lungs. Somehow, I don't think I can manage that. I go to the bathroom and take off my clothes, trying to think of nothing. I'm shaking when I'm just in my underwear and bra. It's not cold. I just can't handle the thought that I'm going to be walking around only in my underwear and scrubs. The underwear is the only sort of reminder I have that I'm still me. It's more of a shame than an embarrassment. I buck up and do my best to make my mind as blank as possible as I unclip my bra. My privacy is completely stripped of me. I feel so vulnerable. I quickly pull on my scrubs. I am still shaking when it hits me that my parents might be gone. I rush back to see them and thankfully they are still there. They are standing though, and my heart sinks because I know it's almost goodbye.

My mom holds out her arms and I barrel into them. I want to tell them how sorry I am. If I could turn back time, then maybe, just maybe, I would have made another choice or even a better choice, although I hate admitting it. When I'm done hugging my mom tightly, I go to my dad and hug him tightly also. When it's time to let go, my arms go limp at my sides. We exchange hugs one last time, but it's hard because my arms are even more limp. We wave goodbye and now I find my whole-body limp. I go back to my room, unprepared for what may happen next.

Identifying Data:

Two days prior to admission [the patient] cut her left wrist twice with a knife and stopped when family came home. It is noted recently she has periods of extreme agitation and being irrational. She has been paranoid. She does not have any friends and has had poor hygiene recently. She apparently recently reported that a ghost was telling her to kill herself. Just prior to admission she was noted to be shut down and she exhibited much disorganized thinking. She has not been eating recently.

[The patient's] parents note that yesterday she was making statements that she would stab herself with a knife or break glass in order to kill herself. She was making sure everyone in the family knew that she loved

them, which concerned her parents that she was possibly preparing for suicide.

What I did when I was in my house just 48 hours ago is as clear to me as the knife was when I saw it through the glass full of water. Water can be clear, but so can the things I want to forget. It's weird how the things I want to forget are the clearest to me. What I did just 48 hours ago is so clear to me it replays nonstop in my mind. It couldn't be any clearer. I was alone in my house. It was Mother's Day and my family was out to dinner. I chose to stay home. It was a spring day, but the air was so hot it could have been summer. The sprinklers were spraying in the distance. The clouds were fluffy in the sky. The dishes were washing in the dishwasher. The washing machine was cleaning the laundry. It was an ordinary day for everyone, it seemed. Well, everyone but me. A song was playing as I grabbed the knife. I could see it oh so clearly through the glass with water in it. If there was anything that wasn't clear, it was my thinking. As I looked at the knife, its blade looked as smooth as the sun glinted off of it through the slanted blinds. The edge was sharp and disturbingly welcoming. I wasn't in my right state of mind if the knife looked welcoming. Nothing would have been like this if I was in my right state of mind. I kept looking at the knife until my breath started to race. Emotions filled me to the point where it was overbearing. The race of my heart caught up with the race of my breath. That race was faster than fast. Something snapped inside of me and I started to bawl uncontrollably. After my bawling slowed down, I took the knife and slit my left wrist

14

slowly, so the blood seeped out with ease. I dragged the knife that was deep in my skin across my wrist. When I lifted the knife up, I saw the blood trailing off my arm. I pressed my lips shut and grabbed a towel to hold it to my stinging wrist. I kept glancing at the driveway to see if one of my parents' cars would turn in the driveway. For a reason I didn't and still don't understand, a part of me hoped they would come and see me the way I was. Maybe I wanted them to see the pain I was in. Maybe I wanted them to know that I was close to killing myself. Maybe I wanted them to remember me when I died right in front of them. Maybe I just wanted them to try to understand what I had become. What had I become? I wasn't sane. I wasn't safe. I wasn't me. How would I describe that? Was I even human? Deep down I knew what I was and what I still am. The word sends shivers down my back. To think it makes my brain yearn for giant boulders to pound it. To hear it makes my ears go crazy with sparks burning to try to slice it. To say it makes my throat fill with boiling bile that wants to burn it into nothing. To think, hear, and say it isn't the worst part of it all. To feel it is the worst part of it all. To feel all of the emotions and everything else that is put together that won't go away. Just knowing that it won't go away is just as bad. I'm stuck with it forever. Forever is forever. That means there's not one minute, not even a second, where I can be free of it.

What I was, what I am, and what I will always be is something called bipolar. When I heard the car come up into the driveway, I snapped totally. Bipolar, bipolar, bipolar, bipolar, bipolar…. It all made sense now. My parents came up the stairs followed by most of my siblings. I froze and the expressions on their faces were so scared. It was the last thing I expected because I thought I was the only one who could be scared in this situation. I threw the towel on the ground as my parents followed me through the door. I started to cry harder than I had before. I couldn't get any words out between my sobs. My dad set his hands on my shoulders and I tried to calm down by taking deep breaths in. I finally could tell them what I was doing. I told them that I was suicidal and that I didn't want to be here. My mom stayed in my room with me as my dad hurried out the door to call my psychiatrist. While I strained to hear the murmured conversation that was going on with my dad on the phone, my mom started to rub my back. When he came back into my bedroom, the expression on his face was deathly worried. I turned my head as my dad told us that my psychiatrist, Dr. Johnson, wanted us to go to her office as soon as possible. I knew she meant immediately, but she was trying to be careful around me. Words and actions. The thing is, she didn't have any idea that these didn't work on me at all. Keeping quiet, I followed my parents outside to the car. When I reached the car, I took one look at my house. I saw my siblings staring at me through the window. I stopped for a second and secretly wished that they would never see me again—partly because I was worried that I wouldn't forgive myself for letting them see me like this, and partly because I was worried they wouldn't forgive me either.

On the way to Dr. Johnson's, I watched the sky go by. It was such a pretty blue. What would it be like to be in the blueness of it all, watching down at my family? Would I go to heaven or hell? Is there even a heaven or hell? I tore my eyes away from it and tried my best to block my mind from any kind of thoughts, whether they were good or bad. It only lasted until we reached Intermountain Children's Home. I hopped out of the car and trailed behind my mom. I knew my dad was behind me. I was in the middle. I ignored the fact that I was being watched like a hawk because my parents wanted to keep me safe so badly. We went up the one flight of stairs and walked into the office I had visited once every month for years. For some reason now, the office seemed oddly different. I should have expected this, I suppose, because this wasn't an ordinary visit.

Dr. Johnson motioned us into her office. I sat down on the couch between my parents. Dr. Johnson sat down in her chair across from us. I sucked in a breath. We started to talk about what happened and if I felt safe. My answer was an honest one: "no." What we began to talk about next caught me completely off guard. Hospitalization was a topic I hadn't even considered. Dr. Johnson turned to me and asked if I thought this would help. I wanted anything that would help. When I said anything, I meant anything. Today was a Sunday and tomorrow being a Monday. My freshman year was over in about two months. Maybe this would mean I wouldn't have to face humiliation over things that I didn't even know. If it was a day off, even then that would be good or great for that matter. I said "yes" right away. I didn't think of any of the consequences. I wasn't sure if this would help, but anything that might help was worth a try. We discussed how my dad would take the day off of work tomorrow to watch over me. This information lolled in my head. I didn't really like the idea of being watched over. Whatever might help though seemed worth it. We drove home quickly while this information still lolled in my head along with the new information that I was going to be hospitalized. When we reached home, I went back to my bedroom and instantly fell asleep.

Each of my siblings came to hug me while they all cried with me until I had to depart from them to go to the hospital. They told me they loved me. All six of them showed how much they cared about me. This was possibly the only thing that made me want to get better. It was such a blessing to have a family like mine, even in circumstances where I was too blind to see it. I did care about my siblings just as much. It was hard for me to show it at times, though. That was because I was so caught up with how to survive the endless pain of my mental illness called bipolar. Hopefully it would all stop once I got out of the hospital. I reassured myself of this, even though the doubt almost overcame the reassurance. I fell asleep deeply throughout the whole night until morning hit. The sun was high up in the sky, but everything was the same. Darkness was still swelling in my heart. My cheeks were dry and sticky from the tears I had cried. I sat up and blinked furiously. I went straight to the mirror, which I knew very well I shouldn't have done. I stared straight at my reflection. My long brown hair was a mess. My bright blue eyes were a dimmed dull. Everything else was either red or chapped. I began to whisper things under my breath. *"You dirty slut, why don't you just go crawl into a hole. You suck and deserve the worst of everything possible. You sickening bitch, go away because no one needs you because you are yourself. You are so stupid, ugly, horrific, and so many things. So why don't you just kill yourself in whatever way that hurts you most. Just kill yourself by overdosing, stabbing, shooting, ANYTHING."*

I used all my willpower to walk away from the mirror. When I did, I glanced at the door, hoping with all my might that no one heard me. Thankfully, no one did. I made sure of it. I opened my door and the aroma of breakfast hit me. I walked into the kitchen to see that my dad was the only one up. I got up on the stool right when my dad turned around. His smile was pulled by an unknown force. It obviously proved it was a fake one, but he was trying hard. I smiled back a forced smile, which was just as fake. We started up a conversation when I noticed that no one else was up. The digital clock on the kitchen read 12:04. It suddenly hit me that my siblings were at school, of course. I felt some giddiness in me that I didn't have to go back to school. I felt like jumping up and down while laughing. When I looked up at my dad and saw his fake smile, all the giddiness slipped out of me. I was instantly reminded of what was going to happen in the next 24 hours. Luckily, I didn't let out any sign of this manic behavior. I ate my breakfast more quietly now. I couldn't tell if my dad was still talkative or not. I just wanted to go into my bedroom and sleep forever. As soon as I could, I went back to my bedroom and lay down. I was about to fall asleep when I felt myself blacking out. It was like my vision could only see black and I knew I was still alive. I screamed for my dad, who rushed over in a heartbeat.

I explained to him about the almost blackout. He sat with me for a while and told me that he would stay just down the hall. I was petrified at what had just happened. I didn't even want to sleep. I tried to relax just as my therapist Marie had taught me since I was in seventh grade. I wasn't sure if this hospitalization would work. Right then I froze. Hospitalization. That didn't mean I had to go back to the same hospital from five years ago, did it? I was about to freak out when I remembered that the hospital I was going to wouldn't be the same one, but was one located in Missoula. I must have been too caught up with the information lolling in my head that my mind blanked out which hospital I was going to. This was supposed to calm me down a bit, but it didn't seem to help at all. I rolled over on my side and fell asleep without almost blacking out this time. When I woke up, it was time to say goodbye.

My older sister came in with my little sister. They both hugged me. My older sister, Megan, smiled and did her best not to break down. My little sister, Ellie, hugged me and her face showed so much emotion, it made me want to cry. We sat down at the edge of my bed. Megan smiled through her tears. It was something I wished I could have done. Ellie was quiet this whole time and I didn't know what to say to make her feel better. We all left my bedroom. My older brother, Danny, was standing in front of me. I was off my feet in one second and in his arms in another second. I hugged him hard and when I looked up at him, he said that he was so sorry if he was ever mean to me. I told him no. He hugged me once more, and behind him were my three little brothers: Paul, Jack, and Nick. My brother, Paul, hugged me once and told me he loved me. I told him I loved him back, but that's all I could say. Jack was next. His curly hair was frizzed up. I smiled on the inside because I couldn't on the outside. He hugged me in loving silence.

My sweet littlest brother Nick was next. He was still in the early years of elementary school and didn't understand most of what was going on. He knew enough to cry into my shoulder. I rubbed his back and kissed the top of his head. As I left for the car to go on the two-hour drive to the hospital in Missoula I took their protective love with me. Without the family I have, I wouldn't be alive. It was their support and understanding that had given me hope ever since the hallucinations first began when I was eight years old and until this hospitalization.

My family and hope. It was what would save me.

Identifying Data:

[The patient's] parents report that she has exhibited episodes of euphoria and grandiosity lasting up to a few hours. She had one episode of going without sleep for 72 hours; this was associated with hyperactivity,

talking faster and nonstop, and significant flight of ideas. She started to exhibit some flight of ideas last night and was singing. She has periods of significant hyperactivity with associated increase in activity level; her activity level at this point is not goal-inherited and she frequently starts things but does not finish them. She has had some preoccupation with sex and recently asked her parents to put her on birth control even though she is not sexually active or planning to be. She dresses in "immodest" fashion. She recently had some rape fantasies.

As I look down at the little menu that serves breakfast, I lose my train of thought because of all the options on it. I remember the only thing that was good at the other hospital was the breakfast in the morning. This breakfast here better be as good. I pick French toast sticks and a muffin with grape juice. In an instant the breakfast cart comes in. I feel a huge grumble in my stomach, which I assume can be heard also. Hopefully I'm the only one who can hear it. Sarah is still here. Hopefully she won't comment on it. Sarah doesn't.

"Here you go," she says, all enthusiastically.

I can't seem to get over the fact of being mad at Sarah. Ever since she told me I can't wear a bra, I hold a grudge against her. She puts my breakfast in front of me and the smell makes my stomach grumble. This is just great. She laughs, and I look down at my food to scowl. I still don't feel comfortable with scrubs, let alone not having my bra on. My face burns when I hear some male voice talking outside. No man better come in here. I know I'm over thinking this too much. I push this out of my mind and eat slowly. My parents just left and with my body feeling limp, I figure food just might help. Eating slowly becomes eating faster. Within minutes I'm done eating. This is an old habit. I eat faster than anyone in my family. I sigh and notice that there are no windows. Sarah comes by and picks up my plate and glass. I don't even look at her. I rest my head against the chair I'm sitting in. I want time to stop so I can just rest. I have a schedule here. I have to wake up at eight exactly in the mornings on weekdays and I only get an hour more on the weekends. Yep I'm serious. That's nine. It's the latest I can sleep in anyway. I don't know why though. Maybe it's to help me not sleep until like three in the afternoon like I always did on weekends at home. Drinking water, eating healthy food, exercising, and good sleeping schedules are the top things to maintain a good and positive life for one who lives with bipolar. Wait, let me rephrase that. It's a life one needs to live with bipolar. Without that, I won't be the happiest person. It may seem easy but it's not. I love juice, not water. I eat things I prefer and not the healthy stuff like vegetables and some fruit. It's harder than hard to exercise when I hate it so much. I'm used to not having a sleeping schedule, and besides, I get jealous when I see that others don't need one. That's another big deal to me. I can't be like everyone else because of my bipolar. I'm different. I'm so different, and I hate it more than anything. I don't know if I'll ever be able to do all of those things. It's taking one day at a time. I lift up my head as Sarah sits across from me with a paper in her hand. I should really expect this, but somehow, I don't.

23

"Emma," she says as she holds up the paper, "this is called a mood chart."

I can't help but make a face. Mood is what I experience 24/7. Why do I have to experience it now? Sarah notices my face and her eyes soften like Dr. Fleed's own eyes did.

"Breakfast was good," I blurt out.

Sarah nods and I feel relief as she turns her attention back to the paper.

"Morning, noon, and evening, you must write how you're feeling, okay?"

I nod and relax a little now that I know what's going on even if I don't like it. It's better to know what's coming than not knowing what's not coming. Sarah starts to explain when I go down to group and when movie time is. I let this information pass although it will stick with me of course.

"There will be other teens in group."

This catches my attention at once. Eh? Other teens? At once I remember I'm still not wearing a bra. I start to feel my face burn up.

"Well, here's the chart. I want you to explain how you feel at this moment."

Sarah slides over the paper to me with a pencil. There's a bunch of smiley faces and sad faces. This is so kindergarten stuff. Sarah gets a Sudoku puzzle book out and I feel a little bit more comfortable that she's focused on something else. I study the chart and discover that this is harder than it seems. I don't know how to explain how I feel. There are too many feelings I feel to write down. I think hard and put down a reasonable answer. I feel that it's hard being away from my family. I put the pencil down and stretch my arms over my head with a yawn. Yes, that's such a good reasonable answer. I'm being honest and as well as not describing in too much detail that will fill up the whole three lines. My handwriting is huge, so I don't have to worry about staying within the three lines or filling them up neatly. Sarah realizes I'm done so she takes the paper. I suddenly feel like I'm being scrutinized closely even though she is just overlooking the paper. When she is done, I follow her back to my room. What she has me do next is even worse than not wearing a bra.

"You need to pee in this cup."

She holds up something that looks like it sits under a toilet seat. No way. Please, no way. This is too freaking unbelievable. I can't take my eyes off what she called the cup. Don't only guys wear cups for sports? I know this is different, but I still can't help but think it.

"Alright, I'll let you do that." She says this before she even sets it on the toilet. When she does and leaves the room, I put my face in my hands, fighting the urge to scream. I'm out of tears by now. I feel frustration and anger filling my head which keeps growing and growing, wanting to erupt. The bad part is that the frustration and anger doesn't erupt even if it's at the highest point. I go to the bathroom and try to pee. It takes a while because I can't really pee if there's noise or I'm being rushed. Now there's another reason why I can't really pee. That is when I'm expected. God, I swear I'm cursed. When I'm finally able to pee and get done, I go to Sarah.

"I'm done," I say, annoyed.

She goes in with gloves on her hands to get the cup that's full of my pee. Well, what did she expect? I snicker as she passes by. Too bad she doesn't notice. Oh well. I rub my temples as the frustration and angriness goes down. Sarah comes back with no gloves.

"Group now," she says with a smile. I groan inwardly. Hopefully no other teens are down there. This is obviously a hope that is impossible. I don't know why I still hope like this. We go to the elevator and down two floors. I cross my arms over my chest as casually as I can. When I enter the room, I see there are two girls and four guys. None of them are in scrubs so I know that there are bras in this room. Just not on me. I sit at the table purposely across from a girl. I'm not sure what comes next, but I sit trying not to think about how red my face is by now, probably even brighter than a cherry tomato. I suck the front of my upper teeth. A lady with short blonde hair enters the room.

"Hello," she says all excited. Looking around the table, it seems that she's the only one who's excited. She turns toward me. "It looks like we have a new member of our group!"

I stop sucking and wave a hand in the air. They all look at me stupidly. Oh damn.

"When we go around the group, let's say our names, alright?" They all nod like robots. They are programmed to know what to do, it seems.

There is one boy who is attractive. I try my best not to stare. His name is Devon. He has skinny jeans and hair that covers half of his face. Oh boy. When it's my turn I flash a false smile.

"I'm Emma."

"And I'm Liz Fleed." That's all she has to say to make me cringe. She is obviously related to Dr. Fleed. She motions to Devon.

"Well," he says. "I have had a good week. There was just one mishap. I drank a whole bottle of cough syrup because my girlfriend broke up with me the other week, so I'll be sleeping alone."

Soon enough I picture myself being that girl sleeping with him. My mind is always doing this. It obsesses with incredible and unexpected thoughts. It's not really me actually picturing myself sleeping with him. It's the thought of it. It's really hard to explain. If someone experiences what I'm experiencing, then that's the only way they will know what I mean. It's disturbing. I remember what Marie called it intrusive thoughts. I try to remember this although it's hard. My intrusive thoughts can be so sickening. Intrusive thoughts include anything. From being raped by my sixth-grade teacher or having sex with someone at least twenty years older than I am who is good to me. When Devon is done talking, Liz gives him the advice of maybe looking toward the positive and focusing on other things. Like that's easy. It's harder than it sounds. Next a girl named Lisa starts.

"My week was fine, but my sister is so pathetic because she tries to frame me in her lies, so I hate her." Lisa has a snotty voice which upsets me all the worse. It doesn't seem humane to say that about a sister. Then again, I know all families are different. I'm lucky to have mine. Liz gives her the advice of trying to talk to someone she trusts. It doesn't matter whether it's not a family member. It should probably be a professional person who can help her talk through it. I now feel even luckier to have the family of mine. When everyone goes around, it's finally my turn. Their eyes feel like daggers. I don't even know what to say. Nothing is really even on my mind.

"I, errr...."

"Just tell us why you're here, Emma."

My eyes water and my palms sweat. My heart beats three times more than normal. I sit up tall doing my best not to start crying.

"I'm here because I felt like killing myself."

I don't mention that I wasn't sure if I truly attempted suicide or not. None of it made sense. Did that mean I was truly a psycho? It comes to me after this questioned thought that the reason why I'm not so sure is because I'm blocking it. I'm blocking what I have tried to do. This is what tends to happen at times when things get too painful. Just at times, though. Now it all comes rushing at me like a tsunami. I wasn't just suicidal. I tried to kill myself. The knife is clear, and the blood running down my skin is clear also. I attempted suicide. The looking to see if my family was coming home soon was more proof that they saved me. How I all of a sudden remember this I have no idea. All this does is makes me ache for my family even more. After all of this, it still hurts but I don't feel like rephrasing what I just had said. Liz nods her head.

"That's why we're here, Emma. We're here to help you get better."

Perhaps this is true. Perhaps this is not true. All I know is that this sounds like bullshit. Without the perhaps, of course. Liz gives more advice and then we all play Apples-To-Apples. I love this game, so I feel a little bit calmer. The girl named Lisa wins. Finally, I feel like I'm actually having some fun. I'm letting myself let go of as much pain as I can. Just by giving myself the opportunity to have fun lets me let go of some pain. When it's over Sarah brings me back upstairs. After ordering and eating my lunch I see the mood chart right by my plate. Sarah returns to her Sudoku and I tap the pencil against the table. I write down right away that I hated telling how I felt but playing Apples-To-Apples was at least fun. Satisfied at my answer, I turn to Sarah who is playing still Sudoku. A smile tries to tug my lips up. I don't fight it. I smile and my God it feels wonderful that's it not unreal. I stop smiling just as Sarah looks up. That's okay for me. Just being able to smile a real smile means I know there's some progress.

"Let me take that," Sarah says.

She reads what I wrote and smiles. She doesn't say anything and that's one hundred percent fine with me. I guess that there are times where I can have some privacy on my own. Even if it's a quick smile it still shows me that privacy exists. It hits me right now that privacy isn't the only thing that exists right now. I, Emma Volesky, exist. That's got to mean something, or am I wrong?

The second night is an okay night. I get to read letters from my family, which makes me know that they still love me. What happened the first night here seemed painful, but the third one is worse. This is an example of how things can change for no reason in an instant. Having bipolar is very unpredictable. I don't know how to put this third night into words. The pain is just what I am basically. I feel no other feeling and wanting to kill myself is the only thought that my mind can process. My brain thinks of knives. The knife I had that cut into my wrist. Well I want that now. I want that so badly right now. Oh, so badly. Just to kill myself to end this torture. I'm sobbing as a new nurse sits beside me. She isn't Sarah, but I don't register this at the moment. Just a while ago I got this new lady and told her I was thinking of breaking my glasses and cutting myself with the edges of it. Now I regret this so bad. I cough on my sobs and what I manage to say is something I want worse than death. I want my mommy. The nurse leads me to the phone and I blink at her. She is an older lady. I don't ask her name because I want to hear my mom's voice so bad. The phone rings and I thank the lord for once that she is the one who answers and not any of my siblings. Her familiar voice makes me hiccup and slow down my sobbing, so I can talk to her. I don't know what I would do if one of my siblings heard me.

"Momma," I cry. She hushes me softly through the phone.

"It's okay, honey," she soothes. I feel like a little baby again, but it can't even bother me. It actually does soothe me.

"Am I in hell?" I ask. "Please, mom, please answer me." She doesn't wait a second in between.

"Yes, Emma, it seems you are."

I let out a laugh, which is a first. This response soothes me more than anything else. I'm almost sure it's because her answers are always right. Knowing that I agree with this one is a good thing. We talk and when I calm down so much more, I finally hang up. I smile weakly at the new lady. It only takes a minute for it to make sense that she is a nurse in scrubs. I should refer to her as a nurse.

"I'm Suze," she says.

I nod, too sick and tired to talk about anything to anyone. I go back to my bed and take deep breaths, trying to clear my brain.

Whatever happened to me? Finally, I fall asleep, thankfully feeling nothing. Not even pain. '

Identifying Data:

[The patient] feels paranoid in school and feels that others are watching her. She then is worried that they are angry with her; sometimes this occurs at home. She becomes nervous in performance situations, but is able to stay in those settings. She denies any thoughts that people are after her. She denies ideas of reference. No thought insertion or thought broadcasting.

[The patient] exhibits paranoid symptoms according to parents. They have had to pick her up multiple times from school because she is convinced that others are talking about her and the voices in her head have told her that too; this also has occurred at home.

The next morning I'm beyond tired. I don't know why this is. I don't know why this is even more when I realize I woke up early without anyone needing to help me. I sit up in bed and lift my messy hair out of my face. I feel better than last night. Suze comes in.

"How are you feeling?"

I look up at her and don't see the soft eyes I see with everyone else. She doesn't even say my name.

"I'm fine, thanks." I actually now have the chance to introduce myself. Even though she knows who I am, she doesn't say my name. I find myself smiling. "I'm Emma."

I brace myself for the response that she already knows, but she says something else completely different:

"It's nice to meet you."

I like how she doesn't say my name at all. It's nice to know that there's at least someone who doesn't say my name within two sentences of meeting me. I get up to take a shower and put on my new fresh pair of scrubs. I go to the mirror and this time I smile at my reflection. It's good to see me smile. It feels good to see myself smile. The way my teeth look white and my full blossomed lips. I imagine myself at school walking the hallways, saying hi to all the teachers and classmates. I don't have issues at all. I can walk the halls without feeling like my every move is being watched and without the fear that everyone is talking about me. I'm wearing cute clothes and no scrubs. I'm normal. I go out the door, which brings me to a parking lot of cars. That's when I stop imagining. I didn't finish Drivers' Ed. I didn't finish that and a lot of other things. I didn't finish my homework. I didn't finish my walk. I didn't finish saying all I wanted to the ones I cared about at school. I didn't finish telling my family that I loved them so, so, so, so, so, so, much. I loved them so much that it couldn't be explained or even imagined. I didn't finish saying that to my family, which was the most important thing. I didn't finish a lot of other things too. I didn't finish my life. When I think about how I didn't finish my life, I find myself still smiling in the mirror. I can't stop smiling and for once I realize that's a good thing.

I gather my pajamas and put them in the required laundry basket. Today I'm actually excited for two reasons. Reason number one is that I get to see my family. I have some uneasiness about it, but I'm so happy. Reason number two is that I'm going to go to group. We're going to be doing crafts today. It might seem like preschool stuff and in a way, it probably is. Learning how to become healthy again means baby steps. It's ironic how baby steps sometimes mean doing baby things when you're not a baby. That's the best I can explain it. I eat slowly, thinking back to when I could barely swallow on the way to Missoula from Helena. I had to force myself to swallow. My milkshake from Wendy's was as hard to swallow as my burger. Luckily by the next morning I could eat normally. When I'm finally done eating, I write down my mood and wait for group. I don't know what changes exactly. I just become excited. Suze takes me down to the group and we all talk about how life is going on this current day. I notice that it seems a lot easier to talk. I can finally believe that progress does happen over time. I know what else is on this current day. Today is May 19th. It's Ellie's birthday. I feel guilty in a million ways that on her birthday I'm in the hospital. If only it was another day, another time, another life. To get rid of some guilt and to make her happy I decide to make two things out of clay. I know one is going to be an elephant. It's been Ellie's favorite animal ever since I can remember. I take pink clay and form the elephant so that it's sitting up. When I'm done forming the elephant I take two little blue beads and put them on its head for two eyes. After that I decide to make a

34

ladybug. I don't know why the idea of a ladybug comes into mind. I rub black and red clay into a circle together between my palms. The ladybug turns out great. Something about it though is too great. I think some and then add a leaf to it. The ladybug is just clinging to the leaf. It reminds me of myself. I think hard about how it does. It hits me hard enough to realize that I'm like that ladybug. I'm clinging onto it, so I won't fall. I'm clinging onto it for dear life. Before, I wasn't clinging to it at all; I just wanted my life to end. Right when I rest my hands on the wooden table, Liz comes by and puts the elephant and the ladybug in some oven to make them hard. I wait and glance over at Devon. He is so gorgeous, but immediately I look away because yet again I imagine myself being that girl he was sleeping with. This disturbs me more than ever and I can't seem to focus. I squeeze my hands together, trying to force myself to not be imagining that. When the oven beeps, Liz brings over what I made. My attention shifts as I stare at them. They turn out better than expected. I let out a sigh. Now it's all a matter of time when Suze comes down to get me. Just when I think this, she enters the room right on cue.

"It's time."

I freeze. I'm seeing my family. I'm actually seeing my family. It feels more real now. Excitement overfills me. I can give Ellie her birthday presents. I can give my family hugs. The best thing of all is that I can tell my family how much I love them. Suze leads me up to the room where people meet to see their families. When I see them, I burst into tears. They are crying too. I don't see everyone but it's enough. I go to Ellie and hand her the presents I made for her. I don't feel the guilt anymore whatsoever.

"Happy Birthday," I say when I hug her. I turn to them all now. "I love you each and every one of you so much." I don't know what else to say. These words give the room a warmer feeling. We only have a limited amount of time to talk. I feel rushed, but I'm glad I get these words out of my mouth. We start to talk about what has been going on at home and what has been going on here. I ask about why my other siblings aren't here. Work and school are the answer. They can't get off that easily. I'm just grateful to see most of them. Time passes by quick and soon it's time for them to go. I feel sad but getting to see my family lifts my mood about ninety percent. "I love you," I repeat, trying not to let my voice rise too high. The excitement is still there. The truth is when I hug them all again before they leave, I don't feel one bit depressed and I'm satisfied about how things went even though the time wasn't very long.

As this fourth day is ending, I get the privilege to wear my bra again. This is the biggest relief I feel yet. I feel like I'm gaining a part of me back. I suppose I am because having a privilege back makes me want to work harder at becoming better. The aftereffect that I experience is that good. I also get to go to the box where I can choose what I want as a nice award. There's not much there, but I choose simple lip liner. It's boring because I know I won't wear it for a while or maybe not even at all, but I don't care. I can at least have something to remind me that I came this far. I slightly smile at this.

I get to watch a movie tonight, too. I go to the area where the TV is and sit down on the floor when two people come into the room. They are both in scrubs like me. I see that one is a boy and one is Suze. This boy is in here like me. We are introduced to each other. His name is Karl. I learn quickly that whatever happens, we aren't allowed to repeat anything that's said in here. It's confidential. I finally find myself able to tell more of what I did. I don't tell the whole story because if I do that, I would be left scarred even more. I think about what would occur if what had happened to me by the choices I made would get out into the world. This chills me to the bone. When Karl and I are done telling our stories, we both agree on the movie *Transformers* to watch. Watching the movie lets my concentration go away for a while. It ends about an hour later. Soon it's time for bed. I fall asleep rather immediately. When I sleep, my mind wanders away, never realizing that tomorrow that I'll see that life is worth living.

It's funny how much some things get you by surprise. A few days have already passed, so it's been a week and I'm feeling better than I have since I arrived here. I go eat and write my mood on the mood chart. Karl is at the table with me. He follows me to group. I study him as I hear him tell his story a second time. I ask myself questions in my head about if he felt the way I did when I first came here. It goes by smoothly, though. I wonder if it went just as smoothly for me in everybody else's eyes. I don't know, and I probably never will. We go back upstairs and when I go to my room, I see pink tulips. There is a card that sits on top of the other cards I have received while being in the hospital. I open it and see that it's from my parents. I read it and smile while I go to smell the tulips. When I go out, I see Dr. Fleed in the hall. I don't even cringe when he leads me to the same room I was in when I first met him. Ashley is there and so are my parents. It hits me that it has been a week. I'm going home today. I'm really going home today. Home, sweet home. The saying never has sounded so true to me. It has never sounded so sweet. Dr. Fleed smiles at me. His smile and eyes don't even seem like the same kind of soft. They aren't a comforting soft or even a reassuring soft. They are more like a proud soft. Like they knew I could do it all along. I put my hands in my lap as I smile at my parents. Dr. Fleed sits down across from me and Ashley takes out her clipboard. I look at the clipboard and it surprisingly doesn't bother me. In fact, it doesn't have to bother me, which is a surprise. Most things usually have to bother me. This shows a big difference than how I was when I first came here compared to how I am now. Dr. Fleed goes through what has happened since I have been here. From the part to where I was so scared of what even the nurses would think of me to the part where I just wanted to stay in bed and not move. I listen intently to this and the things stuck between and not stuck between what happened too. I only fidget a little bit.

38

"Now," he says. "There are some things you need to work on."

I freeze, wondering what in the world that could be. I force myself to meet Dr. Fleed's eyes. He clears his throat loudly.

"You need to work on telling how you really feel instead of trying to keep it to yourself or trying to make people hear what they want to hear. I want you to be honest and do what you have to do to feel better."

This seems fair to me. All I feel like I have done toward Dr. Fleed is dislike him since I came here. I suppose it isn't my fault, given what I have been through, but still. I try to understand that me being here is just to make sure I'm safe. I don't understand it fully, but I have some sort of idea of it. Even if it does feel like a hellhole here, I made it through and I'm going home now. That isn't the plus of it all, though. I barely have the idea of killing myself. Yes, I still feel kind of depressed, but I have become stronger now. Stronger is what matters. I force myself even harder to meet Dr. Fleed's eyes. I take a deep breath in and nod. It's all I can do at the moment. Dr. Fleed returns a nod.

"Does this sound about right, Emma?" he asks. I don't know how to respond in words, so I swallow and just nod again. "Good."

I look over at my parents and don't feel horrible at all. I think back to the times they were there for me. I wouldn't be here if it weren't for them. I'm not talking about the obvious, where I wouldn't be here if they didn't conceive me and I was born. I'm talking about the unobvious. Their nonstop support and unconditional love for me saved me a million of times. It probably saved me even more than a million times. Maybe even like a trillion or beyond. That's what it feels like for me. That's what nonstop support and unconditional love means to me. I smile at them and they smile back. I see the tears are forming in their eyes and I have a feeling it's because it's the first smile they have seen in a while. Ashley keeps writing things on her clipboard. I want to ask if I can go home soon, but I don't. This takes up a lot of wanting but I still don't. When Dr. Fleed is done talking, I relax and try to stay calm, trying not to jump out of my seat.

"So," he says, folding his hands in his lap. "You are free to go."

I feel my own tears forming in my eyes. This is it. I get to go home. I get to go after so much pain that has tortured me. I sniff as I thank Dr. Fleed and I run into my parents' arms. I run to my room and change out of these scrubs that make me feel trapped. When I'm done I look in the mirror. I look profound and new. I'm so grateful that I have made it. The pressure of whatever was holding down on my brain has finally been released. It isn't there anymore, and now I feel sane. I'm not losing it anymore. I'm not as crazy as I thought I was. I'm fine and I survived. When I say goodbye to everyone and walk outside, the fresh air blows my hair. Oh God, how it feels so good. It goes up my nostrils while I inhale and exhale. It's beautiful outside. The heat on my face makes me sweat, but I don't mind it. I love this day so much that I feel that not a whole lot can affect me to make me feel horrible. The day is so beautiful that I admire it. As the stickiness that's on my shoulders fades away an itsy-bitsy bit when I pass some shade under a tree, I see a ladybug on the ground. I smile, thinking of my siblings. I'm so ecstatic to see them. I soon reach the car. I buckle up, as my parents do in the front. I love this so much. I'm full of joy. The car drives away from the hospital and I roll down my window. There is no breeze anymore. It is a spring day. It is a spring day, but the air is so hot it could be summer. Only on this spring day, I plan on being sane.

PART - 2

I can't handle anything. Not the noise, smell, texture, or light. The noise is too loud or is too quiet. The smell is too strong or too weak. The texture is too comfortable or too unfit. The light is too bright or too dim. I'm going berserk. I hate these tight clothes. I don't want to wear socks because they are just too much for me. Where is this coming from? I must have done something wrong. Is it because my mom had to use Tylenol when she was pregnant with me to get rid of her terrible headaches? Is it because I slept two hours every night as an infant? Some family members have issues too. Did I cause my younger brother to have some depression and anxiety issues? Did I cause my younger sister to have some deep depression? Did I cause my older brother to have a history of depression? Did I cause my older sister to have situational depression? I don't know the answers to any of these questions. A humongous part of me is glad I don't. I can't help but wonder, though: if I didn't exist, would things be a happily ever after sooner than expected?

I see these weird sticks. They are distant shadows that move around my bed. I can't breathe when they start to move from the side of my bed, to the foot of my bed, and to the other side of my bed. My eyes are kept open by some unknown force and they can't close. They follow those weird sticks while I wait for them to stop moving. I want them to stop moving so I can breathe again. When they vanish into thin air, I find my ability to breathe freely. The thing is when it's over, I'm not gasping for air. I just lay in bed next to my baby sister Ellie, who is sleeping. She possibly is even dreaming. She can be dreaming of things that don't make any sense to me at the moment. As I stare at her, I make the decision to pull her hair. I want to see if she will wake up. It isn't mean to me. I'm just inspecting to see if she'll wake up or not. It's just a mere interest of what the aftereffect will be. Will her hair be tangled? Will her hair be soft? I want to know, so I take my hands and carefully twist my fingers around a couple of strands of her hair. In that moment I pull down carefully. I freeze when I see that's she still sleeping. This feels like some kind of a challenge now. I pull down hard now without the care. She wakes up at once and starts to cry. I let go and suddenly realize that I hurt her and that I'm going to get in trouble. What I just did was wrong. It was very wrong. I press my lips together desperately wanting her crying to stop. Instead the crying grows louder and louder. My dad comes in and I cower. Ellie tells him what I did, and I try to explain what just happened. I can't get the right words out which gets me into more trouble. My dad asks me why I must do things like this and he reminds me about putting the pillow over Ellie's face the other night. My throat closes up and I turn on my back. I don't want to do this, but what can I do to stop? Before I can sleep I see those weird sticks again. This time I fall asleep before they are gone.

"Mommy," I question in a curious voice. "What are those white creatures moving back and forth between my room and the attic?"

My mom looks at me in surprise. I tilt my head, wondering why she isn't answering. Right when I'm going to ask again, she does answer.

"I don't know." Her voice is faint, but I hear some curiosity of her own.

"I don't want to hurt your feelings, mom," I say when I glance out the window and see my dad coming. "I like daddy a little bit more than you, okay?" My mom nods and I smile, not knowing that this is beyond cruel. I'm only four, but I still don't know. My dad comes into the house and walks downstairs. I turn to my mom.

"I'm tired," I say, yawning. My mom takes my hand and leads me to my bed.

"Good night, Emma."

With that, the door is shut, and I crawl back into my bed. The white deformed creatures return and crawl up across the walls to the ceiling and go past my door to the attic that's closed up. This is what confuses me the most. How can these deformed creatures go into the attic when it's closed up? I don't know, but somehow, they do. I sigh and try to sleep, but I'm bugged that my mom wants me to go to sleep when everyone else is awake. I fight with the options to go downstairs to see what everyone is doing or to stay in bed by myself. I struggle with this too much. I'm trying to force myself out of my bed, when I see more deformed creatures go to the attic. I'm fascinated by this as I watch them keep going. Something about them chills me to the bone, but I'm still fascinated. They disappear and I'm fighting the options that seem to have power over me. Finally, I'm able to get myself out of bed. My mind is bursting with worry that I'll be in trouble. I realize this when I tiptoe downstairs. Confusion fills me when I see most of my family watching a movie. Why wasn't I invited? Do they not like me? Do they not love me? I go into the family room to ask my mom if I can stay up.

"No, Emma." Her answer is precise.

"Why?" My question is just as precise.

"You said you were tired. Go rest, because I think you need sleep."

I go stomp up the stairs with this anger pressuring my brain. I slam my door and bury my face in my pillow. Soon I'm crying hot tears. I hate this. I hate this. I hate this. To learn to hate at four is really unbelievable. That's how it is though. I stop crying and start to grind my teeth together. I don't know how to relax by taking in deep breaths and letting them out just as deep. I just lie here while the pressure keeps building until I see the white creatures again. Their bodies have a texture that I can't describe. It isn't fuzzy. It isn't smooth. It isn't soft. It isn't hard. It isn't spiky. If I reach up, I can't grab the creatures. They are up too high on the ceiling. They are super-fast. I can't blink, or they are gone. Something about them scares me, but I'm too young to know this kind of fear. I'm too young to know that this is a scare that no one else might really experience. I grasp the side of my bed and close my eyes. Just like that I'm asleep. I don't worry at four if they might come back to me. If they do, it won't be a problem because to me they are real. They are real to me, but again I'm too young to know this kind of fear. I don't know the difference. I will only know the difference when I grow up in the next few years to come. When I'm older I will remember these white creatures differently. I will know them being so horrifically deformed because they have no texture and because they disappeared into thin air without a sign where they might be lurking. This is very little compared to what will come next in my life. A turn of events and I will begin to learn that a life can scar even if that scar is invisible.

I want nothing to do with the world. Not at all. I hurt. I hurt. I hurt. Something help me take away the pain. Is that too much to ask? I hold my breath and start to count. Soon I'm slowly losing oxygen. I want to pass out but before I reach that point I open my mouth and gasp for air. My heart is racing and my head hurts way too much. When I stop gasping and my heart race is slowing down I can feel the back of my eyes pricking with tears. To my surprise they don't trail down my cheeks. This makes me even more upset. I don't know what is causing me to feel this way. I don't know why I have to feel this way. I hold back a sob not knowing what else to do. I want something to help but there isn't anything that seems to help. I wail in pain. No one hears me. That's when the tears start trailing down my cheeks.

They leave my face sticky as I slap my face to make them go away. They now leave my hand sticky. I hate the feeling of stickiness. I hate it so much. I brush them off on my pants. They still are sticky. My head falls to my hands. It falls up and down, but it doesn't help. Again, there isn't anything to help. I want to be far away from life. I don't want to be living. I want to be dead. I don't want to exist anywhere. The pain is so intense that I can't seem to move. I shut off my lights and close my blinds. It isn't as dark as I wish it could be in my bedroom. I suck on my upper teeth as the pain increases. It needs to be darker, so I don't have to exist. I glance at my closet. I drag myself to it trying to not be too overwhelmed by the still increasing pain. I slide open the right closet door and slide it shut once I'm inside. Now I can't even see anything. If the pain isn't here I can almost imagine that I don't exist. That's not even close to possible though because the pain is so increased by now that it's eating me whole. I scoot to the farthest corner of the closet. I curl myself into the smallest ball I can. From my neck stretching all the way down to my stomach to my back being arched the way it is makes my whole-body ache. I try to focus on this physical pain instead of the mental pain. The mental pain hurts so much more it practically blocks out the physical pain. I deal with the pain until my parents find me in my closet and see the obvious: I wish I was dead.

I'm washing my hands. I turn on the water. I rub my hands three times together under the water. I shut off the water. I head out the bathroom door only to turn on my heel and start all of this over again.

The faucet has to be on cold because I can stand it better than hot. I don't need soap always. I only need it sometimes. As I am washing my hands under the water for the umpteenth time I see that the backs of my fingers are all wrinkly. They are soft too. They are all wrinkly and soft like a prune. This happens when I take a very long hot shower. I hate this feeling. Still I can't help it. My brain is intent on holding my sanity hostage while it controls me. It makes me keep doing these steps of washing my hands. Repeat, repeat, repeat, repeat, and repeat. When will I have the ability to stop? I keep doing this until my parents come to see why I'm up so late. They are in their pajamas and I realize it must be late at night. I try to find words, but nothing seems to come out. I can't describe why I'm doing this. My mom shuts off the water and leads me back to my bed. Ellie is sleeping and its pitch-black outside as I glance out the window. I crawl into bed and my mom tucks me in. I'm so exhausted and tired. I let out a long yawn. I'm thankful that I'm finally able to stop. That doesn't erase the fact that my fingers are still pruney. It takes me a while to sleep, but when I finally can, I hope with all my might that I won't have to go through this again.

Highs and lows…. Ups and downs…. Very polar opposites…. Unbelievable mood swings…. What does it mean for a child who experiences these things at such a young age? Well for me, it means that these things are just part of my life. I don't know anything else. One moment I'm jumping on furniture with high-pitched laughs that are uncontrollable and the next moment I'm in my bed with the covers pulled over my head, not wanting anything to do with the world. Thinking about how nothing could get worse? Well thinking about how nothing could get worse just makes it worse. At such a young age with these things going on, there's no difference between wanting to live and wanting to die. I'm five when I enter kindergarten. This is a big change for me. Open House was yesterday with the parents and today all the kindergartens are on their own. I sit in the front of the class, eager to see what this school has in store for me. My teacher is a woman with long black curly hair and grey eyes that seem to smile. Her name is Mrs. Turner. She has a very cheery attitude with much care. We start out the year by learning the names of colors and words that the names sound the same with. In other words, rhymes—which I don't learn until later on in the rest of my elementary years. Mrs. Turner holds up a card that looks like a friendly monster that is green. It has a crown on its head and some black shoes.

"Does anyone know what color this is?"

A girl next to me raises her hands. Mrs. Turner smiles in approval. I think this is because the girl raised her hand. I also think this is because the girl has an answer.

"Yes?"

"That's green!" the girl's voice is an excited squeak. Mrs. Turner's smile grows wider.

"Great job, Gina." The girl's name is Gina. I look at her with great interest. Mrs. Turner asks another question.

"Does anyone know what Green is doing?" Another girl raises her hand.

"Is Green walking?"

Mrs. Turner laughs. "Oh no dear she's—"

"Dancing!" I look over to the voice behind me. It's the boy I saw yesterday at Open House, the one who stuck the pink sticker on the board to show everyone his favorite color. There were other kids around him who saw him. They were incredulous that his favorite color was pink. After all, it was a girl's color. I jumped up and tried to correct them. They just stared until they noticed the other activities around them such as the playhouse kitchen or the blocks. The thing that amused me the most about him wasn't that his favorite color was pink or that he knew what the Green monster was doing. No, it was that he had the curliest hair. I have never seen someone with so much curly hair. Mrs. Turner smiled even wider than she did with Gina.

"Great job, Shawn." His name is Shawn. Now I know two kids' names. The rest of the day goes by quickly. This is a new experience for me because no day ever was like this in the past. We kindergartners only go to school for half a day. I had lunch already today before I went through the school doors of Warren Elementary School. Now I wait outside for my mom to pick me up. I sit down on one of the swings when an older kid gets off. I'm lucky because I get the swing before other kids waiting do. I swing high, pumping my legs in the air to make me go higher. I think about what it would be like to be a bird soaring around the world far and wide. I look to my left and wonder what it would be like to be on the Big Kid Playground. I'm going to have to wait until I'm in third grade which is going to take forever, but I don't mind because I can enjoy the opportunity I have now on the Little Kid Playground. That's something that I will greatly disagree with in the future. In the future I will want forever to pass. I will want it to pass until the pain will be over. Little did I know then that forever would take up most of my school years, making me someone people didn't want to be around. The painful school years to come will be forever. It seems like that at the very least.

First grade isn't as welcoming as Kindergarten. I'm sitting in class as everyone sings to Cooper on his birthday. My teacher, Mrs. Nelson, starts the song while everyone else joins in.

"Happy Birthday to you! Happy Birthday to you! Happy Birthday to Cooper! Happy Birthday to you!" The class starts laughing at the end. Mrs. Nelson holds up a finger and starts to add more words to the song.

"And many more on channel four! And Scooby-Doo on channel two!" The laughing grows harder and everyone repeats what Mrs. Nelson has just said. We all clap for Cooper, but there are two kids behind me who are snickering. Polly and Vanessa. They are singing their own version of the song.

"And a big fat lady on channel eighty! And naked men on channel ten!" I frown, feeling upset. Why must they make fun of everything? The truth is my first sleepover was at Polly's house; she lives three streets away from me. My tongue feels thick as I remember it. Polly's stepdad is very cruel. He kept screaming at her. Polly called her mom, practically crying. Her mom's response was an appalling one. She said she was sorry and it would get better. The moment she got off the phone, I had to go home. Now that Polly met Vanessa, they are best friends. They always are together. In other words, their hips are joined. It's weird when they zip their coats together because it reminds me of those joined identical twins on television who were born connected together and need surgery to get apart. It's hard not to be jealous that they are so close. I don't have a friendship like that with anyone. Will I ever have a friendship even sort of like that one? One thing I don't want is an immature personality like they have. It seems like a waste of time. I sigh as Cooper smiles when the song is soon over. We all sit down, and Mrs. Nelson gets a book out. She turns to a certain section of the book we have been working on. There is a picture of Mickey Mouse in a rocket ship, speeding very fast past planets in the vast outer space. Mrs. Nelson tucks her blonde hair that is in a form of a really bad haircut behind her ears.

"Mickey Mouse is looking for Pluto." She holds up the book high, so we can see Pluto, except the cartoon dog is nowhere to be seen. Vanessa raises her hand.

"The cartoon doggy isn't in the picture."

I want to tell her she's wrong, but I don't. I'll just take the satisfaction that she's wrong. To my surprise Mrs. Nelson's lips form into a smile.

"You're right! Pluto the dog isn't in the picture. There is something else called Pluto in the picture, though." My satisfaction slowly disappears as everyone looks at Mrs. Nelson in confusion. "These are planets, as you probably know. The planets have names." Her finger trails through the planets as she says each one's name. The last planet is a small white ball, which I assumed was a star. "Now this is Pluto."

The confusion turns into understanding. Mrs. Nelson goes on explaining how there are words out there that sound the same but can possibly have different meanings. Like wearing a sock or socking someone in the face. Like eating a pear or taking a pair of shoes out of the closet. Like being able to see someone out the window or jumping into the refreshing sea. Even like having different types of swings: the swings on the play set outside my yard or the mood swings that I experience with no idea that they will get a thousand times worse when I'm older. Words can have different meanings. That must mean actions have different meanings too. I wonder which is worse. Maybe it's the whole sticks and stones may break my bones, but words can never hurt me, or maybe it's the whole words hurt but the actions do the showing. Maybe it's a mixture of both of those things to happen. Whatever happens always happens though. There is no difference in that at all because you can't erase what occurs in the past or what occurs in the future.

Second grade isn't as welcoming as Kindergarten either. My teacher, Mrs. Kennison, is an aging lady with huge glasses which make her eyes look like they are inspecting every move all her students make. She doesn't like me very much. I can sense it. At the beginning of the year she seemed a lot warmer. When I wrote A Kid Goes to Jim she nicely corrected me that Jim is spelled Gym. Time passes though and today she seems crankier than ever. I, however, don't really take notice of this until it's too late. I have a lot of questions on my mind. I ask a certain one because it's been bugging me yesterday since my priest mentioned the name Jesus at church.

"Mrs. Kennison," I ask. "Have you ever met someone named Jesus?" She looks down at me and clears her throat awkwardly.

"Uh, no…."

I push this question further. "Is there anyone existing today named Jesus?" She just stares but eventually finds her ability to speak.

"No."

I stand on my tiptoes to ask another question about it, but she beats me to it.

"There are some people who are named Jesus in Mexico maybe…." I smile and the bell rings. Mrs. Kennison looks relieved. I go down and sit in my assigned seat.

"Hello, class." She grins at everyone. Everyone, that is, but me. "Today we will play bingo." The class lets out a hooray. She writes X's and O's on the board.

"I want to be an X," I call out excitedly. Mrs. Kennison whisks around and narrows her eyes at me. I swallow as I see disgust building up in them.

"Emma, you can stay in for the whole recess!" Her voice is tinged with anger. I want to ask why, but I hold back. I don't understand what I have done wrong. Maybe my calling out what I wanted is a little bit out of place. I don't see why I should have a punishment because of stating my opinion, though. I sit quietly through the rest of bingo. When recess comes, Mrs. Kennison sits at her desk and pulls out some papers. I'm still sitting quietly, unable to figure out what I did or didn't do right. Basically, I'm still sitting quietly unable to figure out a single thing.

Third grade is one with much prediction. My teacher isn't like Mrs. Kennison at all and I'm so grateful for that. Her name is Ms. Clarke. She is an older woman but there aren't very many wrinkles.

In the middle of the year when I do something very unacceptable, she lets it fly by. There is a little shop after school called the Candy Shack. You bring quarters and buy candies like suckers and gum. That one unacceptable thing involves the Candy Shack. Ms. Clarke was reading from a book when I realized it was a Thursday. I was immediately bummed once I remembered I forgot to bring money to buy some candy. Without even thinking, I stood on my desk and yelled the most embarrassing words: "DOES ANYONE HERE HAVE MONEY FOR CANDY SHACK?!!!!!" The silence was the only sign of letting me know that what I had done wasn't okay. Slowly getting down off my desk and sinking into my chair, I felt my face heating up. I couldn't look anyone in the eye. I thought back to what I was told when I was younger. I used to go up to people and ask them why they were so fat or that one time when I had my appendix taken out and an older lady was calling for help in her hospital room. That annoyed me, so I told her to shut the hell up. Thinking back to the incident makes me so regretful. Ms. Clarke is reading from that same book today, which is a reminder of what happened. I look down at the desk I'm in, which isn't the same desk I was in during the middle of the year. Even if I know better now, it's still a little unnerving. As soon as Ms. Clarke is done reading the book, we all go to the cubbies to grab our coats. I wait to be the last one and then go outside myself. The sun is glinting harder than ever today, so I have to squint my eyes to see even though I'm not even looking up at the sky. I go to the brick wall off the school and dig my boot into the snow. I'm stuck on the incident still. I start to stomp the snow now as I remember other incidents. I used to waddle around like E.T. *E.T. phone home!!!!* It's what I always yelled while I walked around ridiculously. Even the fifth graders came to watch me after school. They laughed and pointed and told me to do some more. I laughed, thinking they were laughing with me instead of at me. One time in class, I jumped onto the desk and made weird plane engine sounds. I thought I was funny and I thought everyone else did too. Instead all I was doing was making a fool out of myself without noticing it. I clench my teeth together and put my hands over my ears, doing the best to block out the memory of my own voice doing the most embarrassing things.

In fourth grade I finally get to go on the Big Kid Playground. I play on my own on the bars until Polly and Vanessa come to the bars next to me. They are still joined at the hip. They look at me for a moment and then do flips on the bars as if I was just a figment of their imagination. I start to leave when a girl named Evelyn comes to me.

"Can I play?" she asks. I'm stunned. Is this really happening? She smiles, which brings me back to my senses. I smile back at once.

"Yes," I answer excitedly. "Yes, you can!"

We play together and soon the bell rings, signaling class again. I sigh in disappointment.

"Well, bye!" Evelyn waves fast. I do the same in return. I skip to class as my teacher, Miss Atwater, is at her desk on the computer. She stands up and when she sees me, she motions me to come over. I walk over trying to relax my happy jitters.

"Emma," Miss Atwater says sternly. "Did you spit in Wayne's water bottle?" I freeze, the happy jitters becoming nonexistent at once.

"Yes...." Miss Atwater closes her eyes in disappointment. I hate disappointing someone. I can't handle it.

"You know that that wasn't an okay thing to do, right?"

I swallow. "Right."

"So, if you know that, why did you do it?" I think back to how Henry, Rich, and Yvonne said I should do it. It was another failed attempt to make everyone like me. How could I explain this?

"I don't know."

"Please go pull a card." My mouth drops open. I have never pulled a card in any classroom before. It's a mark of bad behavior. Other kids let this go by without much thought. Sometimes they do it over again and again. Me though? There's no way I can put this behind me. I go over to the cards, where every slot has every name of the students in this class. I stare at mine blurrily. I reach out and change the green one to a yellow one. I go to my seat in silence while Miss Atwater starts to talk to us about the spelling test that's coming up Friday. I glance at Henry. He's well absorbed into listening. Next, I glance at Rich. He is just as well absorbed. Lastly, I look at Yvonne. She is staring at me with a smirk on her face. I instantly jerk my glance away.   Immediately, I slink back into remembering what had happened last month. I was going to a sleepover at Yvonne's house in Leisure Village an area a little way off from the school. Leisure Village was full of trailer houses lined up together. Yvonne's trailer was at the end of a long line of them. It was a baby blue trailer with its paint peeling off. My mom dropped me off at the door. It opened, and Yvonne showed up with a wide smile on her face. I gave my mom a forced smile, trying to convince her that I would be okay. Getting the hint, my mom hugged me and drove off. Yvonne showed me around the house just like any friend would. We ate with her parents and her little brother Tony. Things were going fine. That is until Yvonne asked her mom if we could go for a walk. She said yes without looking. I didn't wonder about this. Tony came along with us. When we all stepped outside, I saw it was dark out. The only brightness was the street lights around us. I liked this. The fresh air and the stars were calming. We started to walk further and further away from the house. Uneasiness filled me when there was barely any light at all. We stopped at the park I had seen earlier on the way to Yvonne's. Some person waved a hand up in the air. Yvonne motioned us to the person. I followed Yvonne and Tony reluctantly. The boy introduced himself as Darren. He was thirteen and not in school. We sat around in a circle. Darren took something out of his pocket. I didn't know what it was until he lit it. It was a cigarette. I stilled as he took a long drag. He took the cigarette out of his mouth and blew out smoke. He then handed it to Tony who did the same and leaned over to Yvonne and kissed her. I couldn't help but stare. When they pulled apart, Darren smiled. He asked me to try. Before I could even answer, Tony passed the cigarette to me. I didn't know what to do with it, so I tried what everyone else was doing. I sucked in and coughed at the disgusting taste. I passed it to Yvonne immediately and then tried to guess what I was expected to do. I went to Darren and he pulled me in and kissed me. I was startled when I felt his tongue in my mouth. I pulled back, still startled. Before I knew it, Tony and I were doing the same thing. When the cigarette was passed to me again, I shook my head. Bright headlights flashed in the distance. Darren jumped up and stepped hard on the cigarette that Yvonne had dropped. The headlights came to a stop at the end of the park. A voice yelled out Yvonne's name in fury. Something gleamed in Yvonne's eyes. At first, I thought it was just the headlights, but then I saw deepness to them. The deepness to her eyes was success. It was like she had succeeded in something. We went toward the headlights which came from Yvonne's mom's truck. Tony hopped into the front seat as I followed Yvonne, who sat at the end of the truck. I looked toward the spot where we had been smoking and kissing. I saw Darren's shadow slowly walking away. When it reached the rim of darkness, it fully disappeared. The truck started up and the wind made me chilly. Yvonne's mom picked up speed and the truck kept bumping. I feared falling out of the truck since our feet were out in the air. We hit yet another bump as Yvonne screamed to her mom to stop. I was appalled at how she was treating her mom, who kept ignoring her. We finally reached their house. Yvonne stormed inside, leaving me behind with her mom and Tony. They headed up to the house and I felt unnoticed. I rushed in before the door slammed in my face. The next day I told my mom about what happened, afraid she would get mad at me. She was madder at how they had treated me.

The bell rings and I'm finally able to get up and rush out of the class, without looking back. All I can do is hope that when my parents hear that I had to pull a card, they won't be mad or, even worse, ashamed.

I'm sitting in my desk. I can't tell anyone what I'm feeling. There's no way I can. Why? Well that's because I don't even know what I'm feeling. My mind is reeling, and I can't tell what's going to happen next. I raise my hand high in the air to use the restroom. My fifth-grade teacher, Mrs. Knowles, nods at me to go. I rush to the closest restroom. My mind is still reeling. I suck in a breath. I'm going home. I hate school. I hate it. Besides, it seems way better than sticking around. I have to leave something behind, so no one will know I'm missing. I take off my shoes, thinking people will believe that I'm still around. I don't know that this is something that won't make sense to anyone else. I come out of the bathroom. Having no shoes on doesn't even make a difference to me. I scan both hallways to make sure the coast is clear. When I enter the hall, I start to run. Before I know it, I'm out the door in the cold just in my socks. I start to run faster. Soon my toes are numb. The wintery February weather is a cold rush in my eyes, so I can't stop blinking. My vision is blurred. My heart is beating twice as fast as normal. It's because I'm running and because I'm in an unsure fear. I push aside the unsure fear and start running faster. When I finally have gone down two roads, the unsure fear turns into a sure fear. Did I do something wrong? I reach home, freezing. My mom is on the phone. When she sees me, she practically drops it. Relief and anger are immediately visible in her eyes.

"Emma." She can't get any more words out of her mouth. I swallow suddenly, understanding at that moment that I have made a mistake, a huge mistake.

"I was...." I don't know how to finish my sentence because I didn't know how I was. When my mom gets off the phone, she comes to me.

"You're going to apologize tomorrow."

Tears fill my eyes. I can't do that. I can't go through all the humiliation and guilt. Fury rises within me and I march to my room. I'm so focused on regretting what I did that I entirely forget what I did in the first place. That's what I do: focus on things that aren't the most worrisome instead of trying out what is most worrisome. I never learn what to focus on that will make me feel better. How to try to learn I don't know where to start so I hope no one will ever ask me.

I need to get past this moment. I swallow regret as I enter my school doors. I go toward the front office when I see the secretary, Ms. Neil. I go toward her and blurt out the words I need to.

"I'm sorry for running away!" Ms. Neil doesn't smile but she doesn't frown either. All she does is nod. This is enough for me because somehow when I gain the courage to look into her eyes, I can see forgiveness. Now it's time to go say sorry to Mrs. Knowles. I head toward the hall when a hard, cold voice stops me.

"Emma." I turn around and see my principal, Mr. Hankel, beckoning me over. I follow him into his office. We go over what I did wrong after I apologize to him, too. "Now," he says, "you need to stay in my office for two weeks for detention."

My mouth dries up. I want to plead with him not to give me any sort of punishment like that. I already told him I was sorry. He knows that I know what I did was wrong. Can't he understand that I won't do it ever again? I sit in his office doing homework that Ms. Neil brings in every three hours. It's sad that Ms. Neil has to bring it in herself and not Mrs. Knowles. She must be busy teaching our class, but it seems like she doesn't even want to. How can I say sorry then? Time is ticking away. I hear kids running outside to play from Mr. Hankel's open window. It's tempting to want to go out. I know better, of course. Detention is one of the worst punishments of school. When Mr. Hankel leaves the office for a while I decide to go see Ms. Neil. I need a hug after all. The moment I step outside the office,

Mr. Hankel shows up and glares at me. I want to explain, but no words can come out of my mouth. The next thing I know is that I feel a grip so firm on my arm it hurts. Mr. Hankel steers me back to his office in a rush. I make the choice not to do anything else at all. I don't even explain. For the next two weeks, I'm quiet. Although there isn't a mark on my arm, I can still feel the firm grip. I can't tell which a worse punishment is: having detention which is only for kids who do bad things most of the time on purpose or the grip feeling that probably won't go away for a while even if it's just in my mind.

Finally, finally, finally. My elementary years are coming to an end on this very day. I sit patiently with all the classes in the gym. An assembly is happening. Awards are being given out. I know I probably won't be given an award, but that's okay. It feels like I already have the best award: finally making it through elementary school. I relax when the assembly soon is ending. When it does end, the BBQ party begins. I can't wait to see my parents. They will be so proud of me. I go outside and look around and soon see them. They smile and say exactly what I expected. They are proud of me and that's all that matters at the moment. When the BBQ party ends, I say goodbye to everyone. I leave Warren Elementary School and begin a new adventure toward middle school. I don't have to worry about how bad it will be because summer is around the corner. I love summer because really there's nothing to worry about at all. I get in the car and as we drive away from my now old school, a new feeling of settled peace falls over me.

PART - 3

I shake as I'm writing the note to my family on the floor in the bathroom. It starts out with my dad's name, my mom's name, and the rest of my siblings' names. I write each of them a little personal description. I put all of my effort into it as well as the rest of my energy. In some ways, it's both kind of comforting to write it and really upsetting. Of course, the upsetting part overrides the comforting part more, but they equally have the power to keep me writing the note. It occurs to me as I'm writing that the note isn't just a note. It's a suicide note. This makes me put more detail into it. I hate my bad hand writing and I have the urge to rip it and start over. That's what I always do with other things I write. If it's a story or a poem, every word has to be perfect. There can be no mess-ups. If it's schoolwork and homework, that always is another story. Those types of things I turn in and don't have to worry about anymore. I don't think of this at all though as I'm writing. I'm at the final conclusion of the note now. I'm pressing down hard on the pencil now. It's a mystery how it's not breaking. I tell them I'm so sorry and at the end I say how much I love them. I finally drop the pencil and I'm shaking still. I shouldn't be because I'm finally done, but I am. I close my eyes, steadying my breath. When I open them, I take the note without thinking and knock on my parent's bedroom door. My dad is the only one in the bedroom. He is reading. I shove the note unsteadily in his face. But before he looks at it, I take it and run back to the bathroom. I rip it to pieces in the garbage and fall to the bathroom floor for a moment. I make myself get up and go back to the bedroom. I sit down on his bed.

"I made a suicide note," I say under my breath as tears start to fill my eyes. "I'm not sure whether it's supposed to be true or not, but daddy, I hurt!!!" He looks at me and I'm not able to recognize that he is in pain because I am in pain. His eyes show it, but I'm still not able to. He calms me down and I go to my bedroom, not daring a look to the bathroom where the ripped-up note remains. I try to sleep but all I can think of is when the garbage truck will come and take the pieces of the note far away.

Often, I don't know where to draw the line between just feeling suicidal and actually being suicidal. This is very hard for me to decide how I'm doing. For example, when I'm doing very poorly, and am very depressed, I can't think clearly. Therefore, my mind is everywhere with dangerous questions: should I cut my wrists until there's nothing left but raw skin, or should I stomp on glass shards until I only see blood from my feet? I don't know where to draw the line at all, so it's dreadfully frustrating. The line is so blurry, I can barely even see it. I'm thinking about this after I have caused turmoil in my household. Everyone is tense and stressed. I got yelled at by my mom for calling my big brother saying I wanted to kill myself. I was down because I had no friends to hang with yet again. My mom took away my cell phone. I wanted my dad to tell me it was all going to be okay, but he just gave me a stern look. So here I am as my brain makes everything worse. I have the desire to die. I'm actually thinking of not taking my pills tonight so tomorrow I will feel so desperate for death that it will happen. I'm sobbing as my brain goes on and on with fatal thoughts. I go sit on the floor with my knees to my chin as I wrap my arms around them. I start to rock back and forth. I try my best to figure out whether I'm suicidal or not. I realize though that I have a choice: I can choose to go tumbling down or to go soaring up. This doesn't make things any less difficult. I rock back and forth faster and faster. A little while later I stop rocking and crying, but the pressure is building. This is what it's like whenever I have a meltdown. I have to go through pain and pressure before everything passes. The moment before it passes is the hardest. I hit a brick wall with all these options to choose from. I can't go past the brick wall without picking one of those options. I'm scared to pick an option, though, because it may or may not be the one that's supposed to be picked. If I pick the wrong one, then I'll lose the courage to get out of my hellhole of a mind. The option I pick is to go through the fire of guilt and then go apologize to my big brother along with my parents. I then will have to wait through their "It Is Okays", which may not be for days. I force myself to stand up and go out my bedroom door. My feet are made of steel, but I keep going. I go up the stairs and once I see my mom,

I want to back away. She doesn't say it's going to be okay and neither does my dad. I go back to my room and wish I knew where to draw the line between just feeling suicidal and actually being suicidal, but before I can figure it out I fall asleep. I won't know until later on that that's just it: there is no way to know where to draw that blurry line.

I enter the living room. "Hi, mom."

I leave and then return. "Hi, mom."

"Hi, Emma."

I leave and then return again. "Hi, mom."

"Hi, Emma!"

I do the same thing and the frustration soon becomes known to me. "Hi, mom."

"HI, EMMA!!!!"

I do the same thing one last time, and even though I know where this is all leading, my mom blows up.

"Hi, mom."

"EMMA!!! WOULD YOU STOP SAYING HI EVERY MINUTE YOU WALK INTO THE ROOM!!!"

I bite my lip holding off any words that may start an argument with her. I walk away, still biting my lip. I'm almost to the threshold of my door when I stop biting my lip and run back to my mom. She's recovering from the frustration. I go to her and start to explain. "Mom, I need to—"

"Emma, I don't want to hear it!" I bite my lip again but this time I can't hold off.

"Mom!!! Let me tell you! You always CUT me off!!!!" My mom rubs her temples.

"Lose the attitude, Emma!!! Go." I shake my head but stop before she sees me.

"Leave NOW." I swallow back painful words and let out a groan of my own frustration. I stomp to my room and the thought of saying sorry comes to mind. No, though. The reason I tell myself no is because I'm so angry at my mom and myself. I can't get through the anger. For once maybe that's a good thing. That's because if I do I would say sorry over and over and over and over again. I would say sorry a million times. I don't have the ability to stop repeating myself and I don't have the ability to think of a different way to approach my mom besides saying sorry so much. That would cause the same reaction: her getting so frustrated that I'll have to leave the room. I can't ask her questions to make her feel better because I would ask her the same questions again and again. That would turn into me having the want to ask her if she's mad at me. I would want her to tell me everything is okay and she's not mad, so I can feel better. It would change the whole situation to me wanting to feel better and not her. If that happened I would feel guilty, which would make me feel even worse than before. So instead I drown in my own frustrations of my obsessive compulsive way. I think of the times when I was younger. Just like the hand washing, I also had a frustrating condition called Pica which for me was eating nonfood items like dirt, my blanket, and the wood trim off of our couch. I don't want to know what else is going to jump on me as I enter middle school let alone high school. It better not be harder to work on. I know nothing will be as bad as the delusion and hallucinations of psychosis because I'm on strict medicine. That's the thing though: I can never know.

I close my eyes at once when my little brother Jack yells to everyone that it's time for dinner at the top stairs. I don't want to eat. I don't want to. Well that's partly a lie I suppose. I do want to eat, but not with my family. It's just too hard to sit at the dinner table with my whole family. Everyone usually talks but not me. When I do talk I end up saying stuff that everyone gets upset about. It's better not to talk, I suppose, but when I don't talk I feel the pressure that I don't belong with my family. It would seem like it didn't matter because that way I could just be happy for everyone and just sit to enjoy the conversation. No, though. That's just a description of how a family would be without a daughter/sister struggling with very severe mental illness. I hate this idea, so I go up to dinner and try to sit down with my family. I look out the window and see cars passing by. The cars slow down and the people in them admire our huge, beautiful yard and house. With our wide-open window, they would see our family eating. One chair would be empty of course, after one minute.

Seeing that one empty chair would make the people less interested and speed up their car to drive away. Everyone gathers and sits down. I take a bite of the bread and immediately feel the pressure building. "I'm done," I announce and run off to my bedroom before anyone can say anything. I also don't have to see their distraught faces. It doesn't make sense that their faces are distraught since this happens at every meal. I sit on my bed, and once again imagine what it would be like if I didn't exist. There would be six kids instead of seven. Before Nick was born I would imagine the same thing with the only difference being there would be five kids instead of six. That's the earliest I can remember, although I wouldn't be surprised if this happened since it was just Megan, Danny, and me. If I didn't exist there would be less chaos in the house. Even simple things like eating wouldn't have to be chaotic. If I didn't exist it would be the perfect family. I lie down on my bed and try not to think about how every time I see a car during a meal it speeds away.

Breathe in. Breathe out. Do it again and again. The car is approaching the middle school. It's the sixth graders first day. The seventh graders and eighth graders start tomorrow. This is just a welcoming day for the new kids. Breathe in and breathe out one last time. The car slows down and I hop out. I look at my new middle school. The sign reads Helena Middle School. I feel very jittery. I look around at other sixth graders. Most of them greet their friends from their former school, because they haven't seen each other during the summer but some of them are hanging by the skirts of the school because they feel cautious of this new school and are in fear that they won't fit in. I can relate to that cautiousness and fear. I might even feel it deeper than anyone else around. I begin to walk across the school grounds. I do this because I know my dad is watching me. I go by the tables outside and watch my dad drive away out of the corner of my eye. When I see a student with a shirt that reads Web Leader I relax quite a bit. I had totally forgotten about the eighth graders helping out the new sixth graders out. I will get to see Danny. He's a Web Leader. I silently scold myself for not remembering this. Maybe sixth grade won't be so bad. I gather the courage to go through the school doors now. I follow the stream of sixth graders into the big doors that show the way to the gym. I look around for Danny at once. It's too crowded and everyone gets engulfed into throngs. All of a sudden, I'm overwhelmed, and my anxiety starts up. I look around for Danny again only this time I'm frantic. The throngs turn into groups. I glance down at the papers that by now are way crumpled from my nervousness. I see my group number on it. It's group three. I see a big piece of cardboard box on a stick being waved into the air with a painted three on it. I walk over to it. There are two older boys who are wearing red shirts that read in big letters WELCOME: WE'RE WEB LEADERS!!! I sit down next to a boy with blonde shoulder-length hair and a girl with short black hair that's spiked. I squirm uneasily trying not to be too freaked out by this girl. She's wearing glasses which look way out of place with her spiked hair. One of the older boys starts to clap his hands.

"Hello," he says excitedly. He's very skinny. "I'm Todd and this is Rich." He points over to the other older boy. He's very overweight and waves his hand in the air. "Now we're going to show you around the school." Rich nods in agreement and takes his turn talking.

"We're also going to do games, guys!" Everyone in the groups gets excited at the word games but me. This means interacting with others. I tense and quickly check to see if anyone saw me. No one pays attention, thankfully. I'm not aware that it's even highly unlikely for one to notice another is tense unless their attention is full on the other. Everyone in the group gets up as Rich shows us around the school giving the tour. I do my best to keep my focus on listening Todd and Rich take turns telling us about where to go to our classes, but I can't help but look around for Danny. I start to lose all hope, but when we take a turn I finally spot him. I stop in excitement. The boy with blonde shoulder-length hair runs into me from behind. I don't pay much attention to this. I run over to Danny and give him a hug. He turns bright red and I step back after he doesn't give me a hug in return. He clears his throat and continues to walk. Everyone looks back and forth at us curiously.

"What," I say loudly. "That's Danny, my older brother." Danny walks faster, and he's soon turns into another hallway, disappearing from my sight. My face burns as I hear snickers behind my back. I hold my breath and back away. I return to my group but this time I'm at the end of the tour line. When we go to a certain classroom I can feel everyone's eyes on me now. I'm being scrutinized. I'm being judged. I'm being ridiculed. Now what? Todd smiles at everyone as if nothing happened back there. I try not to convince myself that nothing did happen back there. Todd and Rich soon begin explaining about a game to play with a ball. If someone passes the ball to you, then you have to say your name, elementary school, and what's going to happen at Helena Middle School. Rich holds the ball.

"I'm Rich, I went to Jefferson, and I'm going to make a difference happen at HMS."

He rolls the ball to me. I'm too distracted on everyone staring at me and secretly winging a prayer to God the ball will never reach me that I don't see it stop rolling when it hits my left leg. When all I hear is breathing I look down and see the ball. My pulse races and I make myself say what I need too. My throat tightens as I open my mouth to speak.

"My name is Emma, uh, Warren School, and my big brother beats up anyone who is mean to me so that will happen here!"

My words come out fast and unclear. When I end, I realize by the look on everyone's faces that I'm in big trouble. I swallow and think of something better to say so I can be out of trouble. I can't think of anything though because I'm still trying to figure out what got me in trouble in the first place. It's right above my head but I can't seem to grasp it. Even if I'm able to, it will slip right out of my grasp, just like everything else I need to make sense of so that I know what I did wrong. I'm slow at making sense of these types of things, so it's very frustrating. A teacher is nearby and so is Danny. Right then I know that what I said was very bad. I actually just told my group that my big brother would beat anyone up if they were mean to me. It must have sounded like anyone meant anyone. *Anyone* meant most likely *everyone* at this school. I put my head in my hands. Todd smiles and I'm shocked.

"What was the last part Emmy?"

A surge of relief overfills me. I did speak too fast and too unclear. I speak a little slower.

"I went to Warren and I want to make it through middle school."

Everyone nods, and I roll the ball in a random direction. A girl starts to talk but I tune her out. I still feel everyone paying their attention on me. I don't need to know to look up. What I don't know is that this is all in my brain tricking me to hide away from reality.

Bipolar I, bipolar II, mixed bipolar, rapid-cycling bipolar, cyclothymic bipolar, so many bipolar types. Bipolar I having the most severe symptoms obviously equals me. Of course, that doesn't mean that a person has a lot less harder time than me because he or she was diagnosed with bipolar II or cyclothymic bipolar. That's not the case at all. Right now, though? Well right now I feel that I have the most severe symptoms. I feel that only I have the most severe symptoms and no one else. I have symptoms of both depression and mania. I go from one to the other. I close my eyes and pinch my wrists. I pinch so hard that I flinch. I tense at the pain but keep pinching. I want to die. I want to die. I want to die. The want never stops. When one want ends, another one begins. I quit hoping for the end of it to come because I know there is no ending. I want to cut so badly, but I refrain from doing so. I don't know why I'm refraining. It doesn't make sense that I am. I pinch the hardest yet and I force myself to face the truth. I have a severe illness and it's not going away. I suck in a breath and my facing the truth goes away at once. I'm not brave. I don't have any bravery in me. Will I ever have the bravery to conquer all of this? All of a sudden, a series of giggles escapes my throat. I'm depressed but it's in a funny way. The giggles are too much. I stop pinching and I feel like I suddenly want to fly. I go out into the living room seconds later still having high deals of euphoria. I can't calm down. I see at once that my parents have friends over. I close my mouth in embarrassment. I run back to my bedroom and scream into my pillow. I stomp on the ground in resentment. I take all of my clothes out of the drawer and throw them on the ground. I grab my cell phone and throw it, so it skids to the closet. None of this helps with the anger so I go back to the pinching and the want starts to come again. I have no bravery at all. I just went through my bipolar episodes within minutes. They happened so fast that I can't help but ask myself is there even any time for bravery?

It's moments like now when I think it's probably okay for me to think it's acceptable to commit suicide. I'm sitting in one of my sixth-grade classes as my teacher, Mr. Meyers, talks about whatever he's talking about. I'm trying to figure out what he's talking about. Really, I try. I try so hard, but I can't when my mind is thinking disgusting repulsive things. I'm thinking about Mr. Meyers raping me. I'm not imagining it. There is no image of it at all. Just thoughts are all it is. I can't get them out of my head, though. It's stuck, and there's no escape. It's exactly like mutilating my siblings. Why does it have to be like this? I fight back hot tears, trying not to be distracted. I hate myself so much at this point. The hatred is practically intolerable. I should be grateful for not having the images, but there is no way that's possible. I'm way too young and in too deep to ever start learning about coping with this. I glance at the clock on the wall. Tick, tick, tick. Tock, tock, tock. The seconds go by slowly. I'm at least able to focus on the clock. Not for long though.

"Emma?"

I jerk my eyes away from the clock. Mr. Meyers stares at me through his glasses. I freeze in place. If there's one thing that I have learned over the years in school, it's that most teachers' pet peeves include looking at the clock when it's still class time. Dear Lord, help me so.

"I'm sorry," I mumble.

Mr. Meyers nods, and goes on talking. I will myself not to look at the clock. The bell finally rings signaling for the next class. A humungous wave of relief washes over me. The relief could actually be more than a wave. It could be more like a tsunami. I engulf the sweetness of the relief. I'm the first one out the door and take a deep breath in. Even though the demons of hell will always be in my mind, I at least have the weekend after this day. I won't have to worry about facing the thoughts of Mr. Meyers again until Monday. I go to my next class and see Mrs. Hule. She is talking to Gina, the same Gina I know from elementary school, with a smile on her face. Gina nods along and I can tell she's only half-listening. I stifle a grin and sit in my assigned seat. This class is my favorite because it's all about writing. My finger twitches for the pencil I see on the desk in front of me. I don't have one of my own. I can thoroughly look through my backpack and not find one anywhere. It's typical for me to constantly lose things. I see that there's no backpack beside the desk. I take a look around me seeing no one else is in class yet. I reach over my desk and grab the pencil. When it's in my hands I relax. When I write, the world disappears. I get so immersed in it, that everything else is forgotten, even for a moment. I don't need to think twice about topics to write. I just end up writing. Everyone else files into the classroom and Mrs. Hule begins to explain that all we're doing today is reading the book assigned. I have no interest in reading *The Giver*. There's a really disturbing part in the book where the main character's dad puts a needle in a baby's head. It gives me an icky feeling that makes me want to cry. Things like that make me practically feel like I'm that person. No, not the guilty one, but the innocent one. So instead, I carefully rip a piece of paper from my notebook paper, after making sure that Mrs. Hule is busy at her desk correcting papers. Gina is to my left flipping through the pages in her book. She isn't even reading. I start writing:

> *I'm trying my hardest to not cry and be kind.*
> *The thing is I don't know is how to deal with this mind.*
> *Whatever happened to hellos and not goodbyes?*
> *I wonder how long I can smile behind all my lies.*
> *Why it has to be so hard I don't know at all.*
> *Why won't anyone answer my silent call?*
> *Well this is my life and how it always feels.*
> *My life of pain is slowly turning like wheels.*

I fold the paper and nudge Gina.

"For you," I whisper in my lowest voice.

I smile, and she takes it curiously. I write more similar poems until it's finally 2:45. It's the end of the school. Now it's the weekend. I put everything back in my backpack. I don't even grimace as I put The Giver back too. I jump up and stretch my arms as Mrs. Hule explains we don't have to read this weekend and run out of the class. It was years later that I learned the letter made her cry. I meet my mom and Danny at the car. Danny asks my mom if he can go to his friend Logan's house. My mom says yes after some thought. As we drive away I let the thoughts of Mr. Meyers leave my head.

Yesterday it became very clear that I didn't have friends. The message of why didn't seem very clear. Today, however, the message is becoming clearer. Everyone belongs somewhere. There are these groups. The pretty girls who please most teachers and the guys who play football always hang together. They are all stuck-up and think that they are all that. The girls with too much dark makeup and the guys with the low baggy jeans are always together. They reek of smoke and don't care about anything. There are the girls who are always involved with school activities, and the guys who study hard with big glasses. They think about studying 24/7 and have already decided what college they want to go to. There are a lot of other groups too, that don't stand out too much, so it's hard to describe what they are like and what they do and such. Lastly, there are the others who don't fit in anywhere, and just hang on the sidelines with no one but similar people like them to hang out with. So where do I fit in? I shuffle my feet across the grass wondering about this. In the past I had some friends. I think I did anyways? I look to my left and see two girls from one of my classes laughing together. One is Polly and the other I believe is Renee. I debate whether to go to them. They are very popular. I don't know why I want to fit in with the popular crowd so badly. It's pathetic really. They have specifically high standards. If you don't have those standards, then you don't even go within five feet of them unless there's a few popular people or if there's just one popular person. It's just Polly and Renee. I take the risk and start to walk to them. Before I can reach them the rest of their group gathers around them. I take a step back nearly losing my balance. I walk away in the other direction and try not to look back. Unfortunately, I can't help it. Gina is in the group right next to Polly. She blends in perfectly. I fight back tears and continue to walk in the other direction. As I pass a person I swear I can feel their eyes on me. They burn into my back and I can barely stand up straight. There are whispers too. They are laughing at me. They are all laughing at me. I am different. I am abnormal. I am bipolar. I suck in a deep breath and charge past everyone until I reach the far end of the school. I'm away from everyone. It doesn't help. I can still feel their gazes on my back and their whispers echo in my head like a hammer pounding inside my skull.

I'm home after school. I held it together in school. It's at home where I let it all out. I go into my bedroom and sit on my bed as the tears start to flow down my face. When the tears are gone, and I'm eerily calm I go to the kitchen. My parents are talking and laughing along with most of my siblings. I try to imagine what it would be like to able to join in on the talking and laughing without messing up. I try to shrug this off but it's not a lot of use. I go into the other room, still eerily calm. Today at school I was having a hard time in math class. I was crying because I was so frustrated. My teacher was nice to help me, but I was well aware of how I was the only one who was having this hard of a time. Was I trying too hard or too little? I can still feel the humiliation. Also, today in school Polly stopped by and asked me if I wanted to be her friend. This seemed to be too good to be true. It seemed that way, so I started bombarding her with unreasonable questions like how she knew my name and why she wanted to be friends. She acted perfectly happy to answer but still I was incredibly embarrassed afterwards. Thinking about these things makes me sick to my stomach. The thing that makes me sick to my stomach the most is knowing that Polly probably didn't mean it. I mean why would she, when I'm such a freak? I do my very best to suppress the emotions that are filling me now. Suppressing emotions is way harder than it seems. I am suppressing the emotions so hard that I don't even think of the healthier option: talking about them. The laughter and talking in the kitchen all of a sudden rips me apart. My mind is in a dark place in an instant. My suppressed emotions make me hysterical. I march into the kitchen straight toward the knives and grab one. I make the gesture of stabbing myself in the chest and let out a scream. I drop the knife and run to my room letting insanity take me over yet again.

The whole friend deal; realizing I have no friends is haunting me. I dream of Polly actually being true to her words and of Gina being my best friend. My childhood friend Leah is there along with them. All of them are superior to me. I'm a speckled piece of dust and they aren't even aware of me as they each step on me over and over. Polly is too beautiful to see someone as ugly as me. Gina is too popular now to see someone who was once her friend having such a small profile as me. And Leah is too oblivious to see that I am the same person she once called her best friend. Soon I'm only a particle of dust, because I've been stepped on so much. I wake up with a headache, wanting to cry. Of course, Polly and Gina, but Leah? She doesn't even go to my middle school. She was my best friend. She was there for me when I transferred to the Christian school in fifth grade because Warren Elementary School wasn't working out at all for me. She helped me through Christian school. I think she did, anyway. No, I don't think. I meant to say I know. Why was Leah in my dreams? The headache gets worse as I worry about me and Leah not being friends. No. It was just a dream after all. I close my eyes and try to sleep. I can't, so instead I try to take the parts of my dream to make a better one. No luck because instead they always go back to the beginning: me being that speckled piece of dust.

It turns out I like to pick a fight. Maybe I just find it fun. Maybe I just am too miserable. Maybe I just want my family to suffer along with me. All of these are horrible reasons to pick a fight. I don't really know the exact reason I like to pick fights.

I'm home after another day at school. I'm bored. I want to start a commotion. Any commotion, really. I don't think twice when I'm in situations with other people. Even when I do think twice it still doesn't have a different impact in the end. Either I think too little, or I think too much. It doesn't work any other way. Too little, too much. I find myself grabbing my cell phone and dialing my home phone on restricted. A daring emotion fills me up and I instantly know what I'm doing is wrong. It's very, very wrong. It's dangerous too. My mom answers the phone at once. "Hello?" I form the words to speak. No words come out because my mouth freezes for a moment. My brain is the opposite. It's on full blast. I know exactly what I want to do. For once the words aren't all jumbled up. After the moment passes I put on my best deep male voice. "Are your younger sons there," I growl. "I don't think so because I have them! Ha, ha, ha, ha!" When my mom doesn't respond my mouth freezes again. Only in this moment I can't find any words. It's a second. My mom hangs up and I feel horrible. I drop my cell phone and run the short distance from my room to the living room.

"Mom," I say frantically. "Mom it was me! I was the one of the phone! Mom!"

Disappointment fills her eyes along with some relief that she knows that her younger sons are safe. She still doesn't say a thing. My throat closes up and I struggle to get the words out.

"You knew it was me, right? Are you mad? Are you really, really, really mad?" My mom knows I won't give up without an answer.

"No, Emma, I'm not mad! I'm furious!!!!!"

I shrink away from her back to my room. I don't know why I do things like this when I know the outcome is going to be upsetting to both the person I start a fight with, and me. The person I start a fight with.... Did it actually have to be my amazing mom? I didn't even succeed in starting a fight. What I succeeded in isn't anything close to a fight. Instead I succeeded in making a family member think their worst fear has come true. Whatever I do to make something happen,

84

the outcome is becomes different than expected. It becomes worse or in some situations like this one, the unthinkable. I want to think twice before doing something more than ever now. Too little, too much is there even a way to even it out?

"I swear to you God I will KILL myself if this doesn't go right," I vow a false vow under my breath. I don't mean this. It's more of a huge habit I can't break. Still, wanting to make this special day go right is what matters to me. Every day is a new day as my dad always says. A new look to add to the new day won't hurt. I go to the mirror and study my haircut. Megan did my light makeup. I never fully give myself whole credit for how pretty I am. Well, only when I can be. I usually don't take care of myself. By that, I mean to the extreme. I don't wash my body or hair, I don't brush my teeth, and I don't wear deodorant. All in all, I don't do a lot of things. I put on random clothes and barely brush my hair which I put up in a little bun. Megan took her time perfecting my face with makeup and so I have to take advantage of taking care of myself. Like my dad says, every day is a new day. The day is special for an unnoticed particular reason. It's special because for once I want to try taking care of myself. I want my classmates to see I can be as pretty as everyone else. I can be meaningful in life if I want to be. I may not be great or amazing. I'm for surely not perfect. I'll hopefully be able to reach a point where I can be close to becoming my own type of perfect. Maybe then people will see me as perfect. Hopefully they will. I know that just yesterday I had poor hygiene. I know that well enough. I just anticipate that there is a chance I can be involved with everyone. I'll work on fitting in. I turn my back to the mirror and walk out of the house. As I ride to HMS my anxiety goes way up. No. No. No! I close my eyes as my middle school comes into view.

"Emma?"

I don't even realize that the car has been stopped. I open my eyes and see my dad and Danny staring at me intensely.

"I'm fine," I mutter quickly as if to reassure them.

Yeah right. The only one I'm trying to reassure is myself. I get out of the car and walk ahead of Danny for once. I'm not following his steps or hiding behind his back for once. I try to relax, but my muscles are so tense it's hard not to hunch my shoulders back. I stand up straight and I stop hunching. This feels unnatural because I usually slouch down wherever I am. It makes me tenser. I do my very best to ignore this. I can for now. I automatically stop at the big school entryway. My anxiety has reached its highest peak by now.

"Uh, move it."

I look behind me and see a few peers behind me. I'm blocking the entryway. I step aside as the peers rush pass me. I nearly stumble over. I try to keep my hands from shaking. I put them in my jean pockets only to find none. I look down and see my shaking hands gripping the fabric of my skirt. I let go only to feel my hands shaking the hardest yet. I push the doors without a second thought. I don't want to be late for class. Being tardy isn't a good sign. I reach Ms. Mahoney's class just in time. I look around to see if anyone notices how pretty I look. Even a compliment will be so meaningful. Ms. Mahoney walks into the class.

"Hello," she says in a chirpy voice. "Today we're going to get ready to start some Christmas songs. Fall is coming to an end after all." She smiles wide. Most of us smother a moan, but some immature boys let out false cries. Ms. Mahoney pretends to ignore this but it's obvious she is offended. The boys see this, and their false cries grow louder. I bite my tongue to keep from going over there and smacking them silly across their faces.

"Alright now," Ms. Mahoney says in a determined voice. "Let's practice the levels of our singing." Soon the false cries turned into even into falser howls. Ms. Mahoney pulled down the classroom's projector. I turn toward the boys. One of them is James and one of them is Javier. They are both jocks who play football. They belong to the popular crowd just like the girl Polly who asked if I wanted to be her friend. Suddenly I feel nauseous. A sick feeling overcomes. I look around desperately for a garbage can. When I see one, I lunge for it and sickness fills my mouth. I vomit up what I had for breakfast this morning. When I think I'm finally done, another round of vomit leaves my mouth. This happens repeatedly. Each time I look up at Ms. Mahoney and try to call out to her, I'm interrupted by more and more vomit as it leaves my mouth. I'm in disbelief that she doesn't take notice of how sick I am right now. From the corner out of my eye I see some other teacher walk into the classroom. She sees me at once and rushes over to Ms. Mahoney. When I'm done vomiting I'm taken to the nurse's office. That's not before I hear Javier's horrible comment.

"Ewwww it smells like rotten chocolate!" Howls of laughter fill the classroom. These howls of laughter are the complete opposite of the howls of cries. They are true, not false. The nurse immediately dials my dad's number. When I realize this is happening I shake my head to myself. My dad will think I'm trying to get out of school on purpose again. When he does pick me up he says he understands. It's only when I get home that I realize my effort of looking pretty were wasted. No one even said I looked pretty before I got sick. So much for trying my best.

I'm sweating when I walk into the hospital's front doors. It's time to see my psychiatrist Dr. Relson, and his office is in the hospital. My dad knows I wish I didn't have to be here. As we sit down in the waiting area my dad puts his arm around my shoulders. He doesn't need to tell me it'll be okay. He knows I know that. Still I hate it here. I look around me as I take in the surrounding around me. The smell is a stale hospital smell. It's a smell I smelled not so long time ago, and it's not one bit comforting. I look down at the magazines on the table. The memories still come. They are like ice numbing my brain. I hate remembering. Memories can wash over you and pull you back to the past as if you're reliving it again. This is what happens as I pull a magazine on my lap turning it to a random page. I stare at it pretending I'm reading when actually my thoughts drift my fifth grade hospitalization:

I'm back to being a fifth grader at my house. It was the first time I had seen my parents crying together along with Megan and Danny. Ellie, Paul, Jack, and Nick are downstairs pretty much unaware of what was happening. Danny wasn't holding back his tough attitude. Instead he pulled me into a hug. "I'm sorry for being mean, Emma," he whispered. I titled my head to the side. I tried not to cry, unlike him. Danny was letting his tears fall without the typical toughness of a seventh-grade boy. I hugged him back as hard as I could. I was unstable again. My mom explained that my medications weren't working quite right. I didn't understand this fully, even if I tried hard. The phone started to ring, and my heart gave a lurch. Grandma, grandma, grandma, grandma. I knew she would be calling. My grandma was someone who I loved more than anything. She was the sweetest lady ever. She never, ever let me down. I didn't mean to be irrational when I ran to the kitchen leaving my family for a moment. "Hello," I answered. "Grandma, grandma is that you?" I was shaking so hard that I could barely keep the phone still let alone keep from falling out of my hands. "Yes, sweetheart it's me." By the way she talked I knew she was crying. She couldn't cover it up even through the phone. I knew my grandma too well. She was very important to me and nothing could ever change that. Tears clogged my throat as I realized I wasn't able to see her before I left. I knew why but that didn't make it any easier. My parents agreed my grandma shouldn't see me like this. I knew my grandma agreed to this also. Even I agreed although I tried not to. The last thing I wanted was to let my grandma see me like this. "I love you grandma," I said doing my best to sound strong. My grandma's voice broke then. "I love you too." I smiled through my tears. "Tell Grandpa and Aunt Denice the same please." It took a while for her to respond. I could tell the way she was trying to contain her voice. "I will." "Grandma?" "Yes?" "I love you more!" She laughed a little bit. This counted for something. "Impossible." Her voice was a whisper. I didn't want to hang up. If I could stay on the phone on the same amount of days I would be in the hospital, then so be it. I would take that chance in a heartbeat. It was a wish. The only wish I had right now. My parents appeared, and I swallowed down that wish that I wanted so badly to say out loud. My dad took the phone gently from my hands. I looked away and went to my bedroom. All my clothes were packed neatly in the little suitcase that was placed on my bed. When the suitcase was loaded into the car I knew it was time to say goodbye. Just for a tiny while. My parents and I got into the car. I didn't know what was going to come next. All I could do was look forward to getting me stable on my meds again as my mom has said. Whatever that meant. When we approached the hospital, I became eager. What was this going to be like? I sure hoped it wasn't going to be like the time when I nearly died with my appendix ruptured. That was a true horror story. Nothing could be worse than that. I was almost sure of it. I mean what could be worse than the physical pain of pushing myself, to walk on a medical walker? Little did I know what was going to happen within the next week? I hopped out of the car. I skipped ahead of my parents, so I could reach the hospital doors before them. My dad had my suitcase over his shoulder and I opened the door for them. My smile was wide, and I couldn't understand the pained expressions on their faces. I didn't think much of the expressions. How could I with this new interest? I was just glad to get out of my house because of the depression I was having. The depression lifted a little and I expected it to keep lifting. We reached the front desk and the man behind it and we followed him to another room. To my surprise he lifted some sort of square card to a little black box on the wall and I heard a beep. The door opened and as I went through it I couldn't help but look behind me to see it shut without a beep. It was oddly quiet as we walked down the hall. Soon we finally came to a stop at a desk. A lady raised her eyebrows at us. The man's voice was gruff when he spoke what was written on a sheet of paper. "This is Emma Volesky," he said. "She is here for the short-term unit." The lady nodded and motioned us past her. What did short-term unit mean? I wondered at this. I followed a little reluctant because I saw my mom step back once. She automatically stepped forward as if nothing happened. The lady opened the door the same way the man did with that square card and black little box. This beeped too. She led us toward a desk in the right corner of the hallway. I didn't even notice that it was a room. The only way I figured this out was because the lady shut the door that I didn't see. We sat down, and the lady smiled. I smiled back for only one reason: this place will make me better. She eyed the suitcase that my dad still had. "I need that, so we can mark her initials on her belongings." My dad began to hand her the suitcase but stopped in midair. I noticed he hesitated but no one else did. I felt a feeling of reluctance again. My attention towards that though was immediately disrupted as the lady unzipped my suitcase. My mouth dropped open. I couldn't tell if this was okay to do. It was like an invasion of privacy or something. I brushed this off as if this was nothing. I was here to get better of course. I stuck to this idea as she pulled out my shirts and pants putting my initials on every tag she could find on them. When she pulled out my underwear that's where I couldn't take it. "Why do you have to touch those," I asked frantically. The lady looked up as if she was confused. I swallowed back all the questions I had now. If there was one thing that was really frustrating it was being confused about not knowing what was going on and most of all not being told what was going on. So therefore, I could relate to this lady by being confused but I also felt at fault for not being able to explain. Then again, I was confused too, and she wasn't answering my question. Instead she was looking at my parents who looked just as confused. What were we all confused about? The lady spoke first. "Oh," she said. "It's required here that we put initials on everything the child brings. So, we can know whose clothes are whose." She went back to initialing. The features on my parents' faces soothed out in understanding. I didn't know what my

92

face looked like, but I was not okay with this. Just like I had for most of my life I couldn't say what I wanted to say to state my opinion in what I wanted. In other words, I couldn't stand up for myself even in the tiniest of situations. It was sad really. When the lady was done she looked at me. "Emma," she said suddenly cheerful. "Welcome to." She handed over my suitcase when everything was back folded in its place. It didn't feel the same for some unexplainable reason as I hastily retrieved it. I nodded at her welcoming still frantic. That was all I could do at the very least. Frantically embarrassed that is. The lady got up and looked over our shoulders. She waved someone over to us. I looked behind and saw that it was the same man with the gruff voice. We followed him as he stopped numerous times to put the same square card to different little black boxes. We walked through the doors that I would soon realize were locked from the inside. Soon we came through the last door. What I saw wasn't what I expected. It was a room with a television and small couch with a little area of board games. Off to sides of the room were a bunch of doors. I looked around with more interest than usual. The man pointed toward the closest door to me. "You sleep in there," he said in his gruffness voice. I wondered if it was possible if he could talk in another voice tone. His voice wasn't a cruel gruffness but more like a natural gruffness. I walked through the closest door. It was a room with two beds. I turned to my parents. They smiled but their eyes were watering. Why should they be sad exactly when I was going to get better? I thought back to how I said goodbye to my grandma on the phone just a couple hours earlier. Did this mean goodbye too? All of a sudden, I felt sick. No, my parents couldn't leave yet. They couldn't. How long would I be away? This suddenly all seemed like a bad idea. Yeah, I spent the night at St. Peter's hospital for a week, but they were always by my side. Their eyes weren't really watering at all unlike now. A different lady than before came into the room. "Emma," she said. "We're going to go to watch a movie." My eyes wouldn't leave my parents' watering eyes. I was about to say no when my mom embraced me into a hug. "It's going to be okay, Emma," she said softly. "We'll be back." "When?" "Tomorrow." I still didn't like this answer at all but how could I say no after a hug? After my dad gave me a hug and saying goodbye to both them I followed the different lady. We went to the small couch where there were two other kids that looked around my age. They are both boys. "I'll be right back," the different lady murmured. I sat down on the far end of the couch. The boys were playing a board game. I leaned forward and turned my neck to see that the board game was Monopoly. I used to know how to play. What had happened to knowing how to do a lot of things? I wasn't the girl I used to be. I used to be a girl who was carefree and happy. I was daring and laughed a lot. I remembered that when I went skiing with my family I was always the first one to be at the bottom of the hill first. I used to run so fast that I fell down and had to get stitches in my head. Whatever happened to that girl? She changed when she hit her late elementary school years. Then again was she really all that different from what I am now? Did she just not realize the pain because she didn't know she was not normal? One boy looked up and distracted me from my thoughts. "I'm Jeremiah," he introduced himself. He had a string he was wrapping and unwrapping around his left pointer finger. I couldn't keep my eyes off of what he was doing with the string. He looked down at the string. "You're wondering why I have this huh?" He glanced around at the adults in the room. They were all talking. They kept their eyes on us though I realized. Jeremiah ducked to my height which was pretty short for my age. He took the string and wrapped it around his neck. "I have this in case I want to you know...." He let go of the string with one hand and pulled the rest away with the other quickly because an adult passed us. I was curious now. "I don't know," I said. Jeremiah raised his eyebrows in surprise. "You don't know," he repeated my words faintly. I shrugged as if not knowing didn't have much importance. "Nope." He sighed. "Hanging by my neck. This string is the only way I can kill myself here. I got this string from my sock." He put his feet near me. "See the difference?" I didn't answer because I was trying to make sense of what he had just said. "See one of my socks is shorter than the other because I pulled the thread out." I just stared at him. "Jesus," he cursed in disbelief. "You seriously don't know a thing." He put his feet down. "What's your name," he asked plainly. I couldn't tell if he really wanted to know my name or if he was just dying of boredom. "Emma." He nodded thoughtfully. "Okay, Emma. Why are you here?" I didn't know whether I should answer him or not. The other boy joined in on the conversation. "Give her a break, Jeremiah." Jeremiah scoffed and was about to say more when the different lady that had brought me here returned with a stack of movies in her hands. "I see you've met Jeremiah and Sid," she said suddenly turning all chipper. "Oh, come on, Suzie," groaned Jeremiah. "Another movie?" "Now, now, now Jeremiah. I'll let you pick the movie alright?" Jeremiah scowled but I could see there was satisfaction in his eyes. Sid watched from afar with his arms crossed. He seemed more easygoing. More relaxed. I wondered about this. "Aw come on," Jeremiah said in a forced fussy voice. "Disney movies again? Where are all the R rated movies? At least PG-13?" Suzie held back a laugh. She was supposed to be serious here I guessed. "Ahem," she cleared her throat. "Pick one or Emma will." Jeremiah pulled out Treasure Planet. "This one I suppose." Suzie patted Jeremiah's arm. "Good choice!" "Yeah, yeah," Jeremiah muttered miserably. We sat through Treasure Planet. I grew extremely bored even before it was halfway through. I struggled against this boredom. My mind wandered off, but it always came back when I thought the movie was over. It wasn't even close to the ending each time I did come back. Finally, after what felt like forever, the movie ended. I breathed out a nice long sigh. It was time for some board games afterward. I didn't know how many board games Jeremiah and Sid played during the day. I wasn't a fan of board games, let alone probably doing them more than once a week. After a couple of games, I felt myself growing more and more tired. By the time all of the games were over my eyes were practically glazed of tiredness. I could barely keep my eyes open. The only thing that probably did keep me awake was having to go to the bathroom really bad. I went to the room I was staying in and went to the unknown door that I assumed was the bathroom. I pulled down on the doorknob to find in stuck in place. I pulled up then, but it was still no use. I clenched my teeth in frustration wondering if I was doing something wrong. The different lady came into the room and saw what I was doing. Embarrassed I let go off the doorknob and slunk away from it. "Um," I began. The different lady smiled kindly. "I have the key to open it." This was bizarre to me and when I looked at the doorknob I saw what she was talking about. There was a little straight slot where a key could fit in on the doorknob. The different lady pulled a key out of her pocket. She was about to put it threw the slot when she paused and turned to me. She looked like she forgot to tell me something important. "Emma," she said. "We lock these doors for a reason." I listened intently but none of these words made sense. I wondered if she was going to go on with an explanation, but she was quiet. I didn't know if she was waiting for me to reply or not. I didn't know if I was even supposed to reply. Soon she started to explain although I didn't know why it took her so long to do so. "It's to keep you safe. We don't want you to hurt yourself." I would have burst out laughing if she didn't look so serious. How could I hurt myself in a bathroom? I don't know if the different lady read my mind or not, but she answered the question I just thought. "Drowning yourself in the toilet, doing something with the sink, or anything dangerous." I didn't have any intention of hurting myself. I thought back to Jeremiah and remembered what he said. Suddenly it all made sense. This place was to keep us from hurting ourselves. It was to keep us safe as the different lady had said. I nodded to show the different lady I understood. She unlocked the door when my bladder was about to burst. I went to the bathroom. I couldn't understand why I was here. I mean, yes, I was depressed but hurting or even killing myself? It never even crossed my mind. Now as I was washing my hands I imagined myself putting my head in the toilet bowl to breath in all the water or pounding my skull into the wall. I shuddered trying my best not to freak out. I quickly dried my hands on my pants not even checking to see if there was a towel. I hurried out of the bathroom my mind rushing. The different lady was waiting patiently. I turned my face away from her in fear she would see that I was biting my lip hard. Luckily, the different lady didn't notice a disparity in my behavior. Maybe there wasn't a disparity in my behavior. I yawned just wanting to crawl into bed and sleep. The different lady saw this. "You can change into your pajamas, Emma." I quickly ran to my bag of clothes to see that the bag wasn't there. I turned to the different lady and glanced at her in question. "Let me go get them alright," she said. She walked out of the room and came back within seconds. "Here's your bag." Now I had always been a type of person who hated people being mad at me. I swallowed all the words I wanted to say, afraid I would make somebody mad at me. I started to pull out my clothes when I realized I had to change, but the bathroom was locked, and I couldn't enter it. The different lady was about to leave the room when I stopped her. "Can you open the bathroom door," I asked. She shook her head which made me freeze. Where was I going to change if not the bathroom? Surely not…. Panic rose within me and I did my best to contain it. The different lady tugged her head back toward the room. "Change in here." She left me still frozen. Hopefully no one would open the door when I changed. I started to take off my pants when I saw some red dot shining off the wall. I followed where the red dot was coming from. There was a camera lens in the corner of the ceiling. There was actually a camera in the room where I was supposed to change. I almost marched out the door to tell the different lady that I wouldn't change where there was a camera. I had no guts though, so I held my breath and averted my eyes from the camera. I changed totally cautious that someone could be taking pictures right this very moment. This should be illegal. When I was done changing into my pajamas I crawled into the bed and fell asleep without much thought. I woke up in the middle of the night when I felt wetness under my back. God please no. Please, please, please no. Not again not here. I had issues in the past where I wet the bed. That was when I was younger, of course. I was always at home and tried to avoid sleepovers no matter how much I wanted to go. I got up out of the bed. Why did I have to deal with this? The question was never answered no matter how much I asked it. I sucked in a breath feeling worse than I probably should have. I wasn't a baby though, so it was hard to not feel that way. I remembered that I had to ask to unlock the bathroom and that my clothes were somewhere I didn't know. I stood up straight as tears of humiliation run down my cheeks leaving trails that are stickier than I was from wetting the bed. There was no way of knowing this of course. The humiliation was overbearing so much that I could barely stand straight. I needed to act this was no big deal. I needed to act like this was normal and happened to a lot of people. If only, if only. I peeked out the door for the different lady. She was nowhere to be seen. Another lady saw me and came over to me. "Yes?" I cleared my throat to get rid of the choking tears at the back of it. "I need uh…." I couldn't get words out because I was so humiliated. I just marched back the room with my back no longer straight. It was slumped now unable to be straight. I wasn't even aware that that another lady had followed me. "What's wrong dear?" "Emma." She looked confused. "I'm letting you know my name is Emma." She smiled. "I'm Bea." I couldn't look Bea in the eye even if she was the only adult I knew the name of here. "Now will you tell me what's wrong, Emma?" I looked at the blank wall when I answered. "I wet the bed." The words came out so fast I was sure she didn't even understand what I was saying. "Alright Emma," she said nicely. "You can sleep in the other bed. I'll get you your bag." She patted my back which made me look at her. "Thank you," I whispered. She left the room but not before giving me a comforting smile. It wasn't really that comforting but it was nice to know that Bea put in the effort whether she meant it or not. I finally fell asleep and when it was morning it only felt like I had less than three hours of sleep at the very most. I kept my eyes shut praying that it had just been a bad dream. I counted to seven which was my favorite number which was also my lucky number. I opened my eyes at seven. It wasn't a bad dream after all. I buried my face in the pillow willing myself not the cry. When I couldn't hold my breath anymore I lifted my head up seeing that there were no tears on the pillow. Right when I was finally able to fall asleep Bea entered the room. "Good morning Emma," she greeted me. "Good morning Bea," I greeted her back. My voice didn't sound like mine. It was dry, so I sounded raspy. Bea didn't seem to notice so I presumed my raspy voice didn't sound the same to others. I got out of the bed and stretched. Oh, how it felt good. I followed Bea out the door. I saw a table set out behind the couch I was sitting on last night. Jeremiah and Sid were there eating pancakes. My stomach let out a humongous gurgle because it smelt so good. I joined the table very fervent to eat. Bea put a plate of pancakes to eat with hash browns and grape juice on a tray in front of me. I ate all of it before Jeremiah and Sid finished eating. I averted my eyes from the appalled looks on their faces. I noticed the only thing that was left on my tray was grape juice. My throat was too dry to resist it. Besides it would help with my raspy voice. I drank it but not as fast. When I was done I almost burped. I swallowed it back which made a weird inward sound which I'm sure they heard instead. I looked at Bea. She was busy loading my dirty tray in a rolling bin. I didn't know what was going to happen for the rest of the day. All I knew was that I was aching for home badly. Even though home wasn't even twenty-five minutes away it just might have well been one hundred miles. I had never ached for anything so much in my life or from what I can remember anyways. When everyone was done eating, Bea gathered us to sit on the couch. "We're going to go to the Recreational Room," she said to Jeremiah and Sid. She turned to me. "The Recreation Room is where the games are," she explained. I gave a shrug in response although I couldn't help but feel excited. Both of the boys didn't seem too excited, so my excitement went down a lot. When we got to the Recreational Room the excitement returned. There was a Super Nintendo and a much bigger television. Bea smiled at my upbeat mood. This was going to be great after all. I was surprised that I was this upbeat after all of my depression. "Emma," Bea said. "You can take turns with Jeremiah and Sid alright?" I nodded just eager to go. Bea looked down at her watch. "Half an hour," she said. My face drops. "Just half an hour," I asked. "Yes," Bea answered apparently not recognizing the dissatisfaction in my voice. I try to keep being upbeat but it's hard. When something usually brought me down it was hard to pull myself up. I went to the Super Nintendo still trying to keep being upbeat. I picked a random game and started to play. I wasn't used to this game and only having a half an hour wasn't even enough time to learn. It just felt like a couple of minutes before Sid approached me. I looked over my shoulder seeing him. I wasn't having much fun, so I offered the game control to him. He gave me a half smile and took it. I wondered why he was here and didn't even think of what would happen if I did find out. "What's the reason you're here for," I asked. Sid didn't take his eyes off the screen. "I drank a lot." This intrigued me to want to know more. "How old are you and where are you from?" Sid gave me a sideways glance now. "Fifteen and Butte." My eyes widened. Wow he was way older than me. I wanted to ask more but Bea announced it was time to leave. I decided to save the questions for later on. We all followed Bea to another room which she explained as the Music Room. We were in a line. Bea went first and then Sid and then Jeremiah and then me. I counted each step I made. I didn't want to miscount because then I would get a little bit angry and have to start over again. When we entered the Music Room we remained in the line. Bea wasn't the only adult in the room. There was a much older lady in the room too. She waved at us and rolled out a television. It had a video player. I didn't have any excitement. I mean why would I? The Recreational Room turned out to be totally different than what I expected. I didn't expect anything now. I just wanted out of here. I was missing my family so much. The depression was returning. It didn't make sense how watching me would monitor my meds at all. It never did make sense at all but now I was thinking this was such a waste of time. How was this helping anyways? This couldn't get worse. As the older lady put the video in and turned on the television a show came on. Okay, okay, okay. I was wrong. This could get worse. Music and words came onto the screen. It was a sing-along. I was disgusted. I was in fifth grade not kindergarten. Heck, I was done with sing-alongs before kindergarten. I looked over at Sid and Jeremiah. They were suffering while they sang. I could see it clearly. I started to sing lowly. I wasn't a baby but it sure felt like it. When it was finally over I was relieved. The rest of the day went painfully slow. When it was in the middle of the week a new person came to the hospital. I had learned somewhat more about Jeremiah and Sid. It wasn't much though. I learned there were only a certain amount of questions one was able to ask. Not that that stopped me though. So, when the new person came it was a break from the boredom of everything going so slow that it was torture. It was a girl too. When she was moved I was eager to get to know her. To that point that is. I jumped at the opportunity to getting to know her right away. "What's your name," I asked at once. She wasn't shy at all, but she didn't smile. "Zoey." "Hi, Zoey." "And yours?" "Emma." She nodded thoughtfully. Yay, a new person here. I smiled. She still didn't smile so I cleared my throat and looked away for a moment. A new adult came toward us. I learned after being here a while that there were different adults who came during the day and night. It happened sometimes during the day too. The new adult introduced himself as Luis. We did similar things during the days. My parents came everyday as promised which helped me a lot. It was good to look forward to seeing them. I got reminders of how much I was loved. Like a huge whale quilt my mom made without much sleep. It was put on the bed that I slept on here. It wasn't at all like it would be at my house obviously, but it was just one of the reminders of home. The other reminders didn't have much importance to me, but they were proof that I was not forgotten here. There were even reminders from people who would hurt me for years to come. Like a stuffed purple monkey from my friend I had known the longest who would later turn against me. A book from my aunt who would later become nothing to me. At that moment, though, it meant so much to me. It was two days from me getting to go home when something happened to Zoey that I would never forget. She started to scream while punching and kicking. Luis and another male carried her to a room I didn't know of. It made me stare for the longest time, that I forgot I was playing Apples-To-Apples with Jeremiah and Sid. It was only when Jeremiah cleared his throat that I turned my attention back to them. "What was that?" Sid looked pained as he answered. "They took her in a room to calm her down." I raised my eyebrows. "How do they calm her down in the room?" Jeremiah clucked his tongue, so Sid didn't have to answer. "They leave her in a locked room with a ball for thirty minutes." I furrowed my eyebrows trying to understand how in the world this was supposed to help Zoey. Sid must have read my mind. "I don't get why they do that," he muttered. "It doesn't help at all." I cocked my head to its side. He has been in the same situation before. That night I imagined I was in that situation. It chilled me to the bone so much that I could barely fall asleep. All I wanted was to go home and be away from here. When I woke up the next morning I was still chilled to the bone. This went away instantly when I saw my parents next to me. "Time to go home." My eyes lit up at once. I was ready. It turned out to be worse than getting my appendix out. It was the true horror story of all time. For this and other reasons I promised I would never come back here again.

"Emma?" I look up as Dr. Relson's voice pulls me back to the present. So much for the promise of never going back. We go into his office and I sit on the little couch with my dad. I tell him everything I feel. When we leave, relief doesn't hit me because I know I will eventually have to go back many more times.

We're all watching Bill Nye the Science Guy. I find it interesting but only until about the middle of it. I sink to the bottom of my chair so that my chin is at the desk. I just want to go home. Two classrooms conjoin to watch Bill Nye the Science Guy. This makes me very nervous. I'm beginning to be aware that I can't handle places where there are a lot people. Especially in a small area such as this half classroom filled with immature sixth graders. Boys are snickering somewhere behind me. I feel that they are directed toward me, but I don't know for sure. There are two options at that moment. The first option is to ignore it as if it's no biggie. The second option is to convince myself that they are directed toward me or even worse at me. I sink practically off my chair as if this might help me disappear. The thought that a teacher would tell me to sit up comes to mind, so I sit up. That is only a little bit though. The snickers grow louder. I decide to keep my mind off it by whispering to the new girl, Kayla, who seemed bored too or at least it seemed like that to me. "Pssst," I whisper to get her attention. She looks up from her nails at me. I wonder if she remembers my name. "Yes," she whispers back. I quickly rack my brain for something to say. Before I can say anything the other classrooms teacher storms to us. "Kayla," she barks. I automatically want to save her. It is my fault after all. "It was me, not her," I say loudly. The teacher looks from Kayla to me and back to Kayla again. She shakes her head but leaves us. I sneak a quick look at Kayla. She is glowering at me. I just confessed that it's my fault. Didn't I let her off so why is so mad at me? It is my fault but why isn't she happy? Exhaustion suddenly rolls over me. I'm too tired to think. This time I sink practically to the ground and I can hardly keep my eyes open. I stay like this. If there's one thing I should at least be grateful for it's not knowing that the boys snickering is now directed toward me without a doubt and even worse everyone has their eyes off of Bill Nye the Science Guy. They stare at something else and, yes, that something else they're staring at is me.

So, everyone has an obsession at least for a certain amount of time in their life, and to a certain extent. Whether its cars, music, bunnies, or basically anything else out there, it can be obsessed about. My obsessions are past that which is considered normal. They are considered abnormal. They are considered so abnormal that they freak me out. They are my own obsessions, and they *still* freak me out. Right now, I'm obsessing about wondering what would happen after death. Would there be afterlife? Would there be heaven? Would there be reincarnation? Would there be nothing? I don't know what will happen, but I want to know so badly. I want to take a gun and shoot myself just to see. Yeah, I'm somewhat depressed, but I'm so curiously fascinated about this, that the depression seems like a small part. In other words, the fascination has a greater power over me than the depression. I have the urge just to see what would happen. Would afterlife be wonderful? I mean, in an afterlife I wouldn't be Emma. The mental illness would be gone. That would be a miracle. No more pain. In an afterlife I probably wouldn't know my same family, though. Nope, that crosses out the whole idea of being in afterlife. Heaven would be nice if what believers say is true. It should be better than anything here on Earth. I could even see my dear ones that have already left this world. I would even get to see my all of my family once they pass away. This makes me shiver though. My family passing away isn't comforting at all. The fear of the chance of going to hell makes me want to second guess leaving the world, period. If I would possibly go to hell, well that would be like living with mental illness for eternity. So, no heaven. Reincarnation would be a one hundred percent different experience. There would be a million species to be. From a dolphin to a hippopotamus to a ladybug. Anything really. I could probably be something I never heard of. Heck, I could probably be on a different planet if there's water on it. Would trees count? I try to imagine myself being a tree. No, no, no, no, no. The boredom of it all would kill me. I couldn't be anything else at all. Humans have the most options. That is, except having mental illness, but I couldn't imagine not being able to feel free. The final thought I have comes to mind now. Being nothing.... I can't think at all now. If I was nothing, then it I would never have existed. I wouldn't be able to feel the love of my family. I cringe at this. Thankfully this makes my obsessions stop for the moment. Stopping my obsessions never really happens on its own. I usually need the help of my family to pull me through. I don't know what made me pull me myself out of I this time. That's not my point though. My point is, no matter what, the obsessing most people do is nothing compared to having obsessive compulsive disorder.

I glance over at the clock. It's 5:13. I pulled an all-nighter again. It wasn't on purpose of course. I'm off track in my sleeping schedule. My eyelids are drooping, but I can't sleep. I tried all the different places in my house to sleep. There was no luck. I hate staying up all night and doing nothing. That's where things can get dark. Darker than what's supposed to be the darkest. I dig my nails into the couch as I keep thinking about not being able to sleep. My nails don't get much farther because they are bitten down so short. I shake my head, wanting to sleep. It's frustrating... not sleeping. I flop down on the couch, tossing and turning nonstop. When my body gets tired from doing so, I count to one hundred. I curse under my breath. The worst part of it all is that I have to go to school in less than four hours. I squeeze my eyes shut, dreading the fact that I'll probably fall asleep in class. Stupid, stupid, stupid. Knowing that I have to go to school kills me enough. I hate it so, so, so, so, so, so much. I wonder if it's my doing, or if it's my mental illness doing that makes me despise school. I honestly would love to be dead than attend school. Sleeping forever is a better option than going to school. It seems that way at least. Just as I'm about to finally get some sleep I hear my older siblings getting ready for school. I groan out loud wanting to be dead for sure now.

Megan comes out of her room and stops when she sees me sitting up on the couch.

"Why are you downstairs?" She asks with doubt.

"I couldn't sleep," I answer with no doubt.

She walks to the bathroom to take a shower and I'm finally about to get some sleep again when Danny starts to talk.

"Emma why are you downstairs," he asks with just as much doubt as Megan. I breathe in through clenched teeth before answering.

"I couldn't sleep." I say this with no doubt again. He goes upstairs to get breakfast while he waits for his turn for the shower. The sound of his footsteps reaches my ears. I pull my pillow over my head until it almost suffocates me. I lift it off my head to get air when I can't take it anymore. I'm so tired I can barely keep my eyes open now. My dad comes to find me a little later. I brace myself for the same question. When he speaks it isn't a question.

"Get up and ready for school. It's Friday, Emma. You can get through the day."

I start to complain but my dad is already leaving. If only I can have one second of sleep. I drag myself off the couch to get ready. It's clear to me why I despise school and want to face death instead. What makes me despise and want is both: my mental illness and me. I become conscious that we are attached. My mental illness is who I am. Who I am is my mental illness. We go together with no separation. No separation like spending your life with someone you love by will. Except this is the exact opposite, if not more. The no separation of us doesn't have love in it at all. We are bound by hatred. So much hatred that we can't cooperate with each other at all. The hatred is stronger than anything I have ever felt in my entire life. There isn't an ounce of will in us to separate. We're forced to become one even if that means we kill each other over and over again for the rest of eternity.

I get along with adults better than I get along with kids my age. I never really realized this until my mom once asked my psychiatrist if things would be easier for me once I was adult. Now I'm wondering too, as I sit at a lunch table by some kids who don't even acknowledge my existence. I drink and eat all my food within seconds. This is a mistake because everyone is still eating while all I'm doing is just sitting there. I stare down at the lunch table and try not to blink. There is no acknowledgement. I'm turning my hands over and over. There is no acknowledgement. I start to grind my teeth together. There is no acknowledgement. I roll the balls of my feet quicker and quicker. There is no acknowledgement. None of this is useful and I don't want to make a fool of myself. I take the garbage from my lunch and walk over to the trashcans. I throw it away when I hear people wishing Gerry Holms a Happy Birthday. Two of his friends are trying to make one another sing Happy Birthday.

"You sing it," one says.

"Ha, ha no freaking way," the others says.

"You sing it dude." They laugh over it.

I perceive something totally different than what is really going on right in front of my eyes. I think they are trying to convince one another to sing but they are chickening out. I don't see that they are just joking around with one another. I go over to them.

"I'll sing it!" They look at each other and nod.

"Alright sing."

"Yeah!!!!!"

I take a deep breath in and sing right in front of everyone. I'm shaking more than I thought I should.

"Happy Birthday to you," I sing as everyone turns their faces to me. "Happy Birthday to you."

"Louder! Sing it louder!"

I swallow but raise my voice. "Happy Birthday, dear Gerry! Happy Birthday to you!!!" When I'm done I have the whole cafeterias' attention. My face heats up and I want to disappear. How stupid am I? I need to pretend this isn't bothering me. I start to smile but everyone bursts out laughing. I'm the laughing stock. I can't believe it. I'm the laughing stock. I swallow down tears and go sit back down at the lunch table. Now the kids *do* acknowledge my existence. Only now they scoot away from me as far as possible like I have some horrible disease. Well, I do have one, but it's not contagious as far as I know. When the lunch bell rings I'm the first one out of the lunchroom. By the time school is over my face is still heated up.

I want to be an angel. I want those smooth, feathery wings that no harm can touch so they will be able to soar in the highest skies. I want the grace and the beauty and the perfection an angel has. If I end up being an angel, I would be pure. I will be so pure that freedom would exist. I want to be an angel. I don't want to be a demon. I don't want those scorching scales that can kill because they are too hot. I don't want the evil and the pain and the severity a demon has. If I end up being a demon, I would be foul. I will be so foul that fire will engulf me endlessly. I don't want to be a demon. It turns out I'm neither of these. I'm not an angel unfortunately, and I'm not a demon fortunately. What I am is human. Being human, it's natural to make both good and bad decisions. It's natural to face good and bad issues in life. It's natural to see good and bad in things. What isn't natural about being human is not being able to see every difference between the good and bad decisions. It isn't natural to face both the good and the bad issues at the same time. It isn't natural to see the good and the bad in things to act upon. Sometimes I don't feel like I'm human. During those times, I feel more like a monster. I couldn't be a monster though with this body. I believe I probably feel even worse than a monster. What is worse than a monster? The best way I can portray it is that it's something inside me crawling to get out. It'll do anything to make me let it out, really. It'll make me kick and punch walls. It'll make me let out a bloodcurdling scream. It'll make me plan to hunt down those who hurt me. What could be worse than that? Well, I know actually, but it hurts too much. Still I can't help but let myself know. It's me. I'm the monster *and* I'm the something inside me crawling to get out. It's me. It's all me. There isn't anything worse. I'm no angel because I'm so deeply wounded in the mind that I can't be ever cured. Sadly, I can never be that way, like an angel I'm no demon because I'm so deeply wounded in the mind that can't get any more cursed. I can't ever be that way because guess what? I'm worse. Why? Well that's because I'm human sometimes and other times I'm what I just portrayed. How can I be both? That's what I hope to find the answer to someday. It's in all probability that I won't find the answer, because there probably isn't one. This is who I am as a human and what I am otherwise.

Seventh grade is finally here. That means I have exactly six more years to be out of school. Can I endure that many years? It doesn't matter because I'm practically a walking dead person right now. A zombie, in other words. I enter the big enormous auditorium where all the classes gather together whenever something big is happening. What happens today only happens twice a year. One at the beginning and one at the end. It's called the Bob Pack assembly. It's where the most well recognized kids get the Bob Pack award. I hoped last year that I could be one of those honored kids that are lucky enough to get up there. Last year Danny got one. I was so proud of him. He wasn't just lucky. He deserved it. I gave up on hoping the moment sixth grade ended. School is school. The only thing I can look forward to is it being done. I sit down in one of the rickety wooden chairs that's built into the ground. I don't have any idea of how old these chairs are. I let out a huff and wait impatiently for everyone to get settled in. When everyone is finally settled in my principal Mr. Weber enters the auditorium and walks onto the stage. He smiles wide for everyone. I wonder if that smile is fake or not. I have no idea. Mr. Weber goes into his long boring talk about explaining the Bob Pack to the sixth graders. I slowly fall asleep but only wake up by his booming voice by the next topic. I guess I should be grateful that he's keeping me awake at least. I get really fidgety because I'm anxious for this to be over. The assembly doesn't start until Mr. Weber is done talking. By the time he is done I'm restraining my legs from kicking out to stretch. Damn pill side effectives. I can only restrain them so much. I freaking hate the little aisles between the wooden chairs. Maybe if they were wider I could sideways kick. The wooden chairs are too low for me to kick under them. Soon I can't take it anymore. I do my best to slide down just enough, so I can kick in the room that is under the wooden chair in front of me. It makes a little sound but all the attention in the auditorium is on Mr. Weber who is giving a sixth grader her first award. This doesn't make a lot of sense to me because it's just the beginning of the year. It's most likely the word has been passed on from their elementary fifth grade teachers about how good the students were in the time they were in their class. This makes me want to puke. Not because I don't agree with it but because of my fifth-grade year. The running away from school and hospitalization happened my fifth-grade year. Add the ruptured appendix and transfer to the Christian school. Remembering all of that makes me wish I could tear that year out of history. Since no one heard the small sound of the kick I slide down even more so this time when I do a couple of more kicks I'll have more room to do so. I'll do the next couple of kicks in a row. That way they will go by quicker. I kick a little too hard though and the sound now echoes throughout the auditorium. Mr. Weber is in mid action giving the sixth grader her s Bob Pack award when the sound reaches him. He looks out toward my direction. Everyone is looking my way too. No one but the person in front of me and the people by her know it was me. I try to act just as confused. Mr. Weber blinks three times and turns his head back to the sixth grader. I don't slide down but sit straight up with my eyes on Mr. Weber head. I'm deeply mortified. Knowing I can't slide down to hide my face makes it that much worse. I wait anxiously for the assembly to be over. When it is, I hurry myself out of the aisle. I want to get away from the person in front of me as soon as possible. If she gets a better look at me she will recognize my face for later humiliation. In other words, if she remembers what my face looks like she will point to me and tell people that I was the girl who kicked her chair. She might exaggerate what had happened a bit. While she exaggerates the snickers will arise around me. Imagining this makes me hurry even more. In result of this I bump straight into someone. "Sorry," I mutter and continue hurrying. I don't realize that my feet aren't taking me to my locker like they are supposed to be. Instead they take me to the front doors of the school. I stop at once wanting so badly to go through those front doors. I swallow and turn around and head towards my locker. I don't see anything but my feet because there's no way I'm going to see the faces of my peers. No way in hell am I. When I reach my locker, I look up just enough to unlock the lock. Just when I open my locker I realize I don't need anything from it because it's time for gym. I want to cry. I shut my locker a little bit too fast, so it sounds like a slam. The echo it makes sounds just like the echo in the auditorium. I just stand there letting the echo ring in my ears. I choke down tears as I head to gym. I cross my arms and keep my eyes on the floor. I'm so upset that I don't have even a clue what I might look like to others. With my crossed arms and my eyes on the floor I don't know that I'm giving off the impression that I don't want people around me. I look sour and mad. In a way maybe, I am sour and mad. The impression isn't the one I want to give off. Then again, isn't it always that way? Just like I didn't want the noise to echo, and a million other things isn't it always that way? I always do things I don't want. Whether it's something I know is possible and that I'm aware of, or whether it's something I don't know is possible and that I'm not aware of, it's always that way. That's what makes my life suck.

Death…. Some days I'm scared to think about it and some days I'm not scared to think about it. I toss and turn in bed tonight thinking about death. I debate whether it truly scares me or not. One moment I pray to God that he'll take me as soon as possible. One moment I pray to God he'll let me live a long life. I sometimes ask God if he is going to take my dad soon, take me instead. It'll make sense because I already go through so much pain. Besides if either he or my mom dies, or both of them die then there's a high chance I'll kill myself to be with them wherever they go. I can't live without them. They helped me survive this devastating mental illness and they keep on helping me survive. If they are gone then who will keep helping me? I know they'll leave me someday. Hopefully they'll be in their nineties though. By then I better have my own family. My own husband and kids. Yes, I'll have my siblings but that isn't the same. I can't even imagine what it would be like if my parents weren't here and I didn't have my own family by then. I may be selfish for not being the same. I just can't imagine my life without that perfect someone, and our just as perfect children. It hurts to think about. It really, really does. Maybe when I grow older I'll see I'm happy just being an aunt. Right now, that doesn't even seem possible. Thinking about all of this doesn't help so I toss and turn some more. Before I know it I'm free of whole debate because I fall asleep. It'll come again tomorrow night. All I can do is let my mind go away for at least a little while if not for a long while.

There's always pain wherever I go and wherever I leave. The pain will follow me everywhere. Sometimes it'll get ahead in the front of me. Sometimes it'll get behind in the back of me. I can't outrun it no matter how much I try. I think about this when I force myself to go running on the track outside of gym. I don't want to be the last one again to reach the finish line. I'm already well aware that I am usually one of the last ones to finish every single time. I run with all my might but soon my ribs feel like they are on fire and I swear I taste blood at the back of my throat. I push myself forward and keep running. My head aches and my stomach make me feel like I want to hurl out of my own body. I can't keep myself from looking behind me to see if I'm the last one. I'm not. I can only imagine how it makes me look to others. An insecure competitive freak. I feel like I have to compete though. Not just in running but in everything, basically. From winning any award in school to finishing my test first. It has been like that ever since I can remember. I push myself forward some more, but I can't do it. I stop and gasp for air. My classmates pass me one by one. They don't slow down, but I can feel their eyes on me as they do pass. I get up and start running again. A stitch forms on my side giving me horrible pain. I try to ignore it, but the pain grows more and more. Soon it's practically unbearable to handle. I walk slowly trying to ignore the stitch. No luck, unfortunately. I finish last, as usual. I hate running for a various amount of reasons. Of course, the pain it causes me is one. So is feeling like I'm being observed by my classmates as an insecure competitive freak. Also, just pushing myself, doing my best, has no result in making me be one of the firsts to finish. The main reason I hate it, is just keeping the running routine. I try to stick to running but it never gets any easier. It never, ever gets any easier. Exercising is required when you have severe mental illness. It does help sometimes. I hate it so much, though. The biggest thing that holds me back? Well that's easy: just the fact that running is required for me mostly because I have severe mental illness.

Is it selfish to try to save myself when a lot of people are trying to save me too? I don't know the answer to this. All I know is that I have a different method and a totally different way of trying to save myself than others do. I think about ways to kill myself to comfort me. This saves me from the pain I have to deal with on a daily basis. If I didn't exist, then there would be no pain no nothing. This may seem too extreme for people to even imagine. This probably makes them want to steer away from me. What kind of person thinks about ways to kill herself or himself to not only comfort themselves, but to save them from pain? No one does but a very sick person like me is the honest answer to that question. There are also times where it does the opposite. It destroys me, rather than saves me. It destroys me thinking about ways to kill myself, but I still want to live and exist. It really depends on how sick I am. Sometimes it scares the shit out of me that something so nauseating comforts me. It depends <u>on</u> of what state of mind I'm in. It's hard to figure out what state that is, because I'm so used to both states: wanting to save myself by dying and wanting to destroy myself by living.

I'm so excited. I'm actually going to have a birthday party at the hotel. I invited four girls my age: Leah, Polly, Gina, and my newest friend Chelsea. It should turn out great. I wait on the porch on my house bouncing on the balls of my feet. I can barely contain my enthusiasm that's pumping through my veins.

"Emma," Danny calls from inside the house. "They'll be here soon enough so just come in already." I have to force myself inside. I learned from the last time a friend came over that I should wait inside and not outside at the end of the driveway. It wasn't normal. I don't understand why it isn't even acceptable to wait on the porch. I guess maybe it isn't acceptable. I go inside the house and wait by the window. I don't realize that my nose is practically pressed against the window. When I see the first car come into the driveway I let out a screech. I quickly glance behind me to see if anyone notices the loud noise. Megan and Danny just stare. Doing that is not normal. I have to tell myself this. It's Polly and Gina. She has brought Gina with her? This curious question leaves my mind when two more other cars come in after the first car. My eyes light up. This will be fantastic. The second car is one that I recognize. It belongs to Leah. The third car belongs to Chelsea of course. Polly and Gina come up the porch stairs laughing. They seem to be hooked to the hip, as usual they smile wide when they see me though and seeing that made me feel like I probably could join them at the hip. Well, eventually maybe. I usher them inside. Leah comes up the stairs and gives me a hug. I'm so glad she could come. It honestly is a relief to know someone that no one else at my party <u>knows</u>. That way I don't have to worry about being singled out. I scold myself for thinking this. Why would I have to worry about such things today? On my birthday? It's ridiculous really.

Chelsea then comes up. I give her a hug to welcome her. She hugs back awkwardly. I take a step back embarrassed. I'm usually so huggable to anyone that I forget boundaries. After chatting on the porch for a while my mom announces that's it's time to go to the hotel. We all get into the car and my mom drives us to Red Lion Colonial Inn. We all try to get out of the car at once when we reach the hotel. As a result, we all get all tangled up and burst out laughing. This is what it really feels like to hang out with friends. I never thought there would be a time to have the experience of having fun hanging out with friends. Finally, after we get untangled and get checked into the hotel we sit down in the main lobby. I don't want things to be boring, so I think of stuff we could do. Before I can say the pool is open until 11pm Leah pipes up and beats me to it.

"Let's all go swimming," she says with bright eyes.

The girls all agree by nodding to what she has just said. I'm about to say that's it's open until 11pm but Leah beats me to this too.

"It's opened until 11 tonight girls! Let's go!!!!"

Everyone runs to the room where we're all staying. I'm the last one and try to keep up with their pace. I notice that Chelsea is not ahead of me like Polly, Gina, and Leah are. I slow to a stop and look behind me. Chelsea is walking slowly. She seems to be enjoying it even. This confuses me. Wouldn't she rather be with the other girls than the one left behind by herself? I walk backwards until I am next to her. I smile but then remember the award hug. To my major shock she smiles back.

"Are you ready to go swimming," I ask carefully.

Her smile fades a bit it's still there. "Sure," she answers neutrally.

I decide right then that I will help Chelsea feel more welcome. How I could do that I don't know yet, but it will happen. I promise Chelsea in my head that she will have the best time like I'm going to have. No wait. I mean like I already am having. I shake my head wondering why I just thought that. I had laughed in the car just moments earlier. I haven't been able to laugh like that in the longest time. When Chelsea and I enter the room all the other girls are already in their swimming suits. I try not to feel hurt that they didn't wait for us. They're already set to go into the pool. Chelsea doesn't seem put off about this like I am. I hurry off to the bathroom to change into my swimsuit. Ever since I can remember, I have been self-conscious about my body. I don't like it even when there isn't anyone to compare my body to. I sigh in remorse about my feelings towards myself. I notice as I put on my bikini bottoms that I have just started my period. I cluck my tongue in disgust because I don't have a tampon. I put my head out the bathroom door and call out to anyone there. Chelsea comes in the direction where I am. Only Chelsea I notice.

"Uh I need," I mumble embarrassed. I can't finish because I feel my face flush bright red. I don't need to look into the mirror to confirm this. Chelsea leaves me and I'm in shock. Should I have sent her an invite to my birthday party? I squeeze my eyes down hard that I don't realize that Chelsea is back.

"Emma?" I open my squeezed eyes at once. Chelsea is right in front of me.

"No one has any tampons," she says in a low voice. She says it in a low voice because she knows if she says it loud I'll feel even more embarrassed. I swallow feeling shame come over me. How did wondering if I shouldn't have sent her an invite cross my mind? "Is something bothering you?" Chelsea asks in concern. I shake my head. Of course, I do that. I hide my mistakes a lot. In fact, I don't even care anymore. Everybody sees my insecurities enough so why let them see more? It's better to hide everything. No one will know how sad I am inside. Chelsea looks at me intently but doesn't say anything. For that I'm grateful. "Let's go see if there's anything in the front desk that could help," she suggests. I start to say no automatically but she's already out the door. I can't help but smile a bit. I follow Chelsea and we reach the front desk. I take a step back even though it's a lady at the desk. This is so mortifying. Chelsea just opens her mouth. "Are there any tampons," she asks with no hesitation. The lady nods and hands a couple of tampons to Chelsea. "Thank you!"

"You're welcome."

Chelsea turns to me. I'm frozen in admiration.

"Let's go. We don't want to miss swimming now, do we?"

When I'm in the bathroom and am done getting ready, I let Chelsea have a turn in the bathroom. I find the right words to say. "I really appreciate what you just did for me." Chelsea nods as if it was no big deal to her as it was for me. "Of course."

I go and wait by the rest of the girls. Gina seems to be sharing a story about some guy that has Polly and Leah laughing their heads off. They don't even notice me as I sit down on the bed. Gina continues the story, but I barely listen. I just drift off in happiness that I invited Chelsea. When she comes out of the bathroom Leah is leading us to the pool. I feel like I'm the one who should lead us to the pool because it's my birthday, but I guess life doesn't work that way. I don't go right away. Instead I lack back in the line with Chelsea. We share friendly smiles.

"How did you know about?" I don't need to finish my sentence for her. She knows where my sentence is heading at. She shrugs in response.

"How do you handle the situation?"

"I carry them around a lot and they last for me."

"Lasting how long? You don't mean you keep them in for more than four hours."

"Yeah I do." I stop in middle of my tracks as she says this.

She looks at my expression and laughs. "It's rare to have toxic shock syndrome."

I nod saving my next question later for my mom. This topic is a pretty personal one. We reach the pool and I see the girls splashing each other and laughing. I can't convince myself that I'm having the best time. I'm too hurt. My gaze goes to the ground as tears purposely fill my eyes. I brush them away quickly as I feel Chelsea's presence.

"I'm sorry," I whisper. I shouldn't have whispered or even answer for that matter though, because my voice becomes croaky with the clogged-up tears in my throat.

"Don't be." She really doesn't want me to be. I smile but not enough. Chelsea joins me now. I expect this very much so. I have already learned much about Chelsea within limited time. It feels so good, but that doesn't mean the hurt disappears to a great extent. Leah goes to dry off and I look up and see Polly and Gina getting ready to jump into the pool. Together without me. I press my lips together wondering when they would take in that I was right there wanting to join oh so badly. Their countdown to jump enters my ears louder than it should have. I drop my head, so my hair falls over my face. I don't want them to see my eyes that have started to purposely fill up with tears again. They probably won't notice that the tears are falling down my face by now. Is it possible for them to care? Do they want to care? I sigh as I sit down on the edge of the pool with my feet dangling in the water. I imagine myself sinking to the bottom and not coming up. If I ended up drowning would that make them care? I shudder at this and hurry out into the hallway. I don't understand why my brain has to do such horrible things. It disturbs me to the point where I need to get away from what it's making me imagine. This doesn't help at all. I make it possible for me to get onto the ledge of a window in the hall. This is not the time to imagine such things. It's my birthday for, God's sake. If it is though, why does it feel so wrong to be here? Chelsea stands in front of me.

"Are you okay?"

I think about being honest for a second, but my answer is a lie.

"Yes, I am." I know that Chelsea knows I'm lying. I'm appreciative that she doesn't point this out. I'm in too much pain to explain, let alone say much otherwise. She stands in front of me still, because there's nowhere else to sit. I'm too selfish at the moment to stand beside her so she doesn't have to be alone standing. I don't know if it's the pain or just my nature or something else that makes me selfish. I don't know what it is, and I don't even care. Not even caring is proof enough that I'm selfish. I don't know how long I sit and Chelsea stands in silence. It's only when I hear the other three girls coming into the hall that I hop down and greet them like nothing is wrong. Like I expected they don't notice that I have been crying. We all go into the room and celebrate my birthday with cake and presents. When everyone is falling asleep I promise myself I will apologize to Chelsea for making her stand and not saying anything to her for the rest of the night. I just hurt so much more afterward when Polly, Gina, and Leah didn't notice. I fall asleep numb from the chilling thought of how I imagined me drowning myself just to see they would care. When it's morning I sit up to see Chelsea gone. I start to panic but then see that Polly and Gina are gone too. What the heck? Polly comes in sight with Gina and Chelsea. My eyes grow wide when I see they're set to go somewhere. Even Chelsea.

"Where are you going," I ask all of them, but my eyes are on Chelsea. Gina answers.

"We're going to a game Emma! Thank you so much for inviting us!"

Polly smiles sincerely. "Yes, we had a lot of fun."

Chelsea smiles. "It was nice hanging out with you Emma." All I do is nod robotically. I'm still halfway asleep. They all leave, and it occurs to me that maybe they really didn't know how I was feeling throughout my birthday party. If so would it still be their fault or mine? I hear the door click shut and I realize I'm still staring at the spot Chelsea was at. It hits me that I probably didn't make Chelsea have the best time. I screwed it up. I let my hurt overcome me and now it was too late to apologize. Chelsea has already left. I know that I don't have control over making Chelsea have the best time, but I still tried so didn't that matter? No, it didn't because I didn't try enough. I feel a pit of regret in my stomach for not trying as much as I should have. Leah wakes up right then and sees me feeling sad. She sits next to me. I wait for her to pull me into a hug. Just as I start to wait my mom comes in the room. She hugs me before Leah does. I embrace her forgetting that Leah was about to give me a hug. No one gives as good as hugs as my mom. It doesn't even occur to me that the obvious would make sense to everyone but me as usual. Leah was as rude as everyone else. Going ahead and not waiting for me is a perfect example. When my mom lets go of me she brushes my hair out of my eyes.

"Don't worry Emma," she says. "Family is here."

Leah clears her throat. "I am too."

I wait for her to give me a hug now that my mom let go of me. She doesn't. I'm too shocked and hurt about the others leaving that this doesn't matter to me at all.

"I'm going to have to take you two up to the Great Divide to ski," my mom says excitedly. I sniff and swallow down the tears that are clogging my throat.

"Yes, that would be good mom," I respond hoarsely. My mom smiles and I do in return. We drop Leah off at her house and go home. Later on, during the night I'm not able to sleep. I go out to the living room and see that my dad is still up. He is working on the computer for his presentation tomorrow. I sit down, and he feels my presence. He looks up from his computer. "I can't sleep," I say. There is no smile like I expected. Instead I see sorrow in his eyes. "How are you doing," he asks. I raise my eyebrows.

"I'm fine...." My dad stands up from the chair he is sitting in and goes to the couch. I follow him. We both sink into the couch.

"You can't sleep because of how the girls treated you." I look at him and sadness fills me as I remember. It becomes clear that what my dad has just said is the reason why I can't sleep.

"Yes, dad, yes." My voice is small as I tell him this. He hugs me.

"I'm so sorry this happened to you Emma-Lou-Boo." I'm so sad that I don't even smile at my nickname.

"They hurt me." To say this makes me feel free of some of the pain that I feel.

"I know." I try to force a smile, but my lips are too chapped. Even if they weren't chapped I probably wouldn't be able to because my whole face is used to one expression: blankness. I try to keep my face blank, so no one can tell what I'm feeling. I rest my head against my dad for a while. I keep it short because my dad has to get back to his presentation. I sit up. "I'm going to go to bed now. Goodnight daddy."

"Are you sure you can sleep?" I shrug and start to leave but stop when I realize something.

"Thank you." My dad looks confused. "Thank you for comforting me. I do feel better."

My dad does smile now, and I go to my room. What I realize is that it's okay to say what I feel at certain times. It feels good. I'll face them tomorrow and tell them how I feel. What I don't realize is that it's not going to be easy. Instead it will be a thousand times harder. I wake up the next morning feeling nothing like I did when I fell asleep last night. Just like almost every morning I don't want to get out of bed for school. This morning is so much worse. I stay in my bed until Ellie pulls the blankets over my head.

"Emma," she says impatiently. "Dad has to take me to school too you know!" I cringe at the word school. I start to pull the blankets over my head but let them drop from my hands. I can't ignore this forever. I get up and hop into the shower. I let the water wash over me. I take the quickest shower ever. I don't have time to think much. I would have loved to take a longer shower, but school will start in less than half an hour now. When I dry off and put some clothes on I drag myself down out the door to where my dad and Ellie, Paul, and Jack are. Ellie will be in sixth grade next year and Paul is a fourth and Jack is in second grade. I get in the passenger seat and realize a difference at once. I feel tension in the car about what had happened even though it's supposed to be the opposite because they know. They are trying to be nice. I got in passenger seat and the door was even open waiting for me. I don't slam the door, but I shut it hard. This is a bad idea because the tension grows. I clench my teeth. We drive in silence. My dad drops off my three younger siblings at Warren Elementary School.

"Bye," they all say at once. I slouch down in my seat as we drive on into town. I close my eyes and try not to think of anything. Just when I think I'm succeeding the car lurches to a stop. I sit up at once.

"Bye dad," I say trying to sound that I will be fine.

My dad just nods. "Have a great day."

I don't say anything more. I go up the stairs of my middle school. I'm almost to the top when I stop dead in my tracks. Gina's locker is right next to mine. How could I forget about all of this? I swallow, wishing at once that I just stayed in bed. I take baby steps to my locker not giving a shit today that people might be looking at me weirdly today, which is something that I usually worry about every day. Gina isn't there. I highly hope that she is sick today, so I won't have to see her. By the time I reach my locker Gina still isn't there. I do the code on my lock. To my shock it doesn't unlock. After two more tries and still not opening it I wonder if I lost memory of the code. I shake my head to myself. I may have lost my mind but not my memory of something so simple. After one more try I get it right. I swing open my locker and grab my books. It swings back just when I'm done grabbing my books. I'm that quick. I'm about to walk to my first class when I see Gina right at her locker next to me. I freeze for a moment. When I unfreeze, I expect myself to walk away but I don't. Gina turns to me but doesn't look me straight in the eye.

"I forgot your present," she says. "I'll bring it tomorrow."

I nod and decide I will wait for the present. I go through school trying to not think about what had happened just the weekend before today. I see Polly who waves to me with a smile. She turns to her other friends. I wonder for a quick second if she really has no idea what I have been feeling. That's only for a quick second though. Gina knows. I'm aware of that because of the way she didn't look at me straight in the eye. I breathe out a sigh of relief when I'm out the school doors. I go home and just tell my parents I made it through. I tell them that everything is going to be okay. The present never came the next day though. Or the next, or the next, or the next for that matter. It never came at all. Throughout all of this there is one thing that I think I learn: finding true friends isn't going to be easy.

If there is one thing that I'm one hundred percent grateful for, it's by far my family. I love them more than anything. I'm leaning toward believing that they save me every day. It does make sense the more I think about it. Take my parents for example. They never give up on me and raise me with so much love just like they do with my other siblings. They care for me so much and never stop. They are very understanding no matter what and are always putting my needs first. If there is one thing they do that stands out the most to me, it's that they keep up with my struggles. They never get behind on my mood swings and are always at my side when I feel suicidal. It doesn't matter if my highs and lows are that bad. It doesn't matter if the suicidal feelings are only there a little bit. They never get behind. They even sometimes get ahead of my struggles. This amazes me. How do they do it? I don't ask myself this a lot because it doesn't matter. If the question does enter my mind I wonder but it just passes. I know why. It's because my parents love me. They love me no matter what. When I was younger I asked my parents if I killed someone and went to jail would they still love me.

I didn't say that on purpose of course. To them I made it seem on accident. They said they would love me no matter what. Killing on purpose or accident I didn't know what I meant by that. I knew I wouldn't kill anyone on purpose or by accident. I know at this moment I don't have to ask my parents if they love me that often anymore. If I do, it's very little. My way of asking now is saying I love you and seeing if they say they love me back. I had to use killing as a case in point for my parents to make sure they loved me was because I was sick. I will always be sick. Yet my parents will always love me. Take all my siblings for another example. Well, a different example. They love me. I know they do but they just don't show it much. Maybe it's because they aren't mature enough? That's possible because they aren't grown up totally. One benefit of my mental illness is that through the pain I have learned much. In other words, I matured in a different way. I'm still immature in a lot of ways, but I'm sure I understand what pain is through life, more than they ever will. Maybe it's because they don't know how to prove it to me like I expect it? I do blowup at even the littlest things that set me off. They don't know how to react to these blowups. I wonder if that's because they're cautious or worried. They have to be careful around me. They are afraid for me. As I wonder about this more, something stands out to me. They are afraid for me. That's just sad. That's so sad. Why would they have to be afraid for me? Because they love me? Yes, that's most likely why. It doesn't explain why they don't show it though. How does that work? They are afraid for me.... Or is it also of me? This questioning has the ability to shoot fears throughout my body. Isn't it questionable for a sister or brother to be afraid of you? Not always. Yes, this scares me, but other wonders fill my head. If they were scared of me, that doesn't mean they don't love me. Megan does so much for me. Danny does too. So do Ellie, Paul, Jack, and Nick. Why do I have to doubt that? That's just it. I don't have to. All of my family helps me no matter what. They saved me a million times over and over again. I realize then they weren't afraid of me but what my mental illness might do to me.

I go to class after lunch. I hate this class especially. Mr. Stevenson is the reason why I hate it most of all. He is mean, mean, mean. I don't get why Mr. Weber would even hire someone like Mr. Stevenson. He should fire him. Megan had him when she was in seventh grade. Her story about the experiences she had in the class makes me sick to my stomach. Mr. Stevenson's method to humiliate his students hasn't changed since my sister left. I know this because the humiliation was just as bad as it is today. Megan described her story with much honesty. Honesty is a good thing usually but hearing stories like Megan's makes honesty hurt. Just like my class today, Megan's class had to stand on a chair to read. In front of everyone.

Megan's story goes like this: there was a very overweight boy who was very quiet and started to mumble out of the book we were reading as a class. Mr. Stevenson told him to stand up on the chair so that everyone could hear him. The boy froze at this. Mr. Stevenson glared at him hard. When the boy stood up on the chair it creaked, and he wobbled a bit. He tried to keep steady, so he wouldn't fall off the chair. He didn't, which was a good thing. If he did fall off Mr. Stevenson would humiliate him even more. The boy read louder but with a bright red face. There were a few snickers here and there but mostly everyone felt so bad for the boy their mouths stayed shut. I don't know if Megan stood up for this boy. Now that I think about it, I should have asked. Mr. Stevenson passes out a test. I don't look up because I know what these tests are like. I had one of them before. If you want extra credit you have to stand up on your chair and shout what it says in the paper. It's easy for most of my classmates to stand up on the chairs and shout whatever. For the rest including me, it takes a lot of guts as well as the expectation of embarrassment. What makes it worse is that his tests are the hardest thing I have to deal with for school. I can do anything else like projects, homework, etc. Tests though, not so much. The worst types of tests are timed tests. I don't have to deal with them a lot. Everyone finally is in the classroom, so the test begins. I start to do the multiple choices and fill in the blanks. The questions that one has to recall from memory to answer is what kills me the most. Before I start, my classmate Lance stands on the chair and shouts out, "Mr. Stevenson is the best teacher anyone could ever ask for!" My jaw drops open. How in the world am I supposed to say the same thing? It's a lie and I'm not supposed to lie. This is too horrific. I shut my jaw and try to remember the questions I have to recall. It requires much more thought now that I know that I'm going to have to shout the most sickening words ever. When I can't recall much, I just write down my best guess. I look down at what is at the end of the test. Yep, the words to shout out are there. I know I'm going to have to say it if I want a good grade. I need the good grade because I'm 90% sure that I failed the test. Right before I stand up another classmate shouts out. Then another and another and another. I wait for my turn as more and more go. I just want to get it over with. I stand up in my chair and look down. This is a huge mistake because right when I start to shout it out another classmate says it louder than me and drowns my voice out. As I force myself to look up my classmate has already sat down. I'm standing there like an idiot. I try to say it, but everyone is staring at me. I clear my throat and say the lie under my breath. I sit down immediately. My face is as hot as an oven turned on high. Mr. Stevenson announces that the test is over. We all stand up just as the bell rings and set our tests on his desk. I place mine on his desk and hurry out of the classroom. I head to my next class trying not to think much. I don't realize that by the time I reach my next class I'm holding my breath to the point where I'm about to pass out.

If there is a point of forgiveness in life, I don't know it. I'm not talking about not knowing how to forgive others. No, that's easy. I forgive easier than I forget. I'm talking about forgiving myself. I don't forgive myself. Hell, I can't forgive myself. It's not only difficult. It's impossible. I hope that one day that there will be a possibility to forgive myself. The question about it is, is it my fault and not my mental illnesses' fault? It's too hard to know. I have so many faults and misgivings. I hurt people around me with my selfishness. I'm usually forgiven by others but that isn't the same as forgiving myself. I blame myself. People tell me that I'm the strongest person they know, but I have a hard time believing that. People tell me that they can't go through what I go through. People tell me that I can't be a more beautiful, compassionate human being, but I can't see it at all when I look in the mirror. I can't make sense of this. If I ever say these things or anything similar to myself, it will be a sin. I try not to sin. I do sometimes, but not about this. If I do sin about this, I will never face the fact that there might be hope to get better. I will live in the shame of it. What is even worse is that if it were ever possible in the future to forgive myself I wouldn't. I couldn't take that free pass of forgiving myself. So, I give all my might and effort not to say those things. No matter how tempting it is I will NOT say those things. Even if the world is ending I won't. If I think those things, it's different than saying them. My mind can't help to think things I don't want it to. This is especially if I tell myself not to think certain things. Like the horrid thoughts. If I'm walking downtown and see an older teenager than me riding a bike I hope he will run into a wall. This comes to my mind automatically and there's no way to stop it.

Nothing can stop it. It's something that I can't help. That's why it's different when I think it. Not that I don't feel horrible after it. I feel so horrible after it. I still don't forgive myself. Again, the question about it is, whether it's my fault or my mental illnesses' fault? I feel that it'll never be known because my mental illness keeps me from ever knowing. It holds me back from knowing. I pray that's it's my mental illnesses' fault. Then maybe it's okay if I never know. If it's my fault, I can't help but want to die. This is another reason why I can't forgive myself. Welcome to my life of not having the ability to forgive myself: a life of blaming, a life of hurting, a life of never getting what is wanted: a mind free of everything that a mental illness can rob of you.... Even simple forgiveness.

Pill type one, pill type be done. Pill type two, pill type screw you. Pill type three, pill type leave me. Pill type four, pill type dumbass bore. Pill type five, pill type eat me alive. Pill type six, pill type ignorant mix. Pill type seven, pill type false heaven. Pill type eight, pill type ugly hate. Pill type nine, pill type poisonous wine. Pill type ten, pill type stop when???? Since I was eight years old I have been on numerous types of pills. Not only the types of pills but each pill itself sucks. I wish each pill would be done with its side effects. I wish each pill would screw itself over and over again. I wish each pill would be boring dumbasses, so I wouldn't have to take them. I wish each pill would drown in its own ignorant mix. I wish each pill would burn in hell aka the false heaven. I wish each pill would die from being so hatefully ugly. I wish each pill would be poisoned from wine. I wish each pill would stop all together at exactly when I say. I wish all of these upon them because I want to be able to live without the worry of forgetting to take them each night and morning. I don't know what would happen to me exactly if I went off my pills, but I wouldn't take the chance. If I take the chance I would have no control whatsoever. I wouldn't be me. At least I don't think I would be. I just don't know. I want to be just like any other teenager so badly. The pills are yet another reminder that I'm not normal. Then again do my pills make me normal because what they do is make me stable? When I'm stable I'm sane. Or at least I think I am. There are so many questions that I want to figure out. That I wish to demand answers from. I WANT ANSWERS!! Even one answer would make a huge difference. Is that too much to ask? Pills are why I survive. They are what keep me surviving in everyday life. Still the questions are there every time I swallow my pills. All the pill types suck. All the not knowing what would happen if off the pills sucks. Everything about pills just sucks. Which leads to the biggest question of all: would it actually be worth not taking them?

The worst part of a new semester means walking into at least one new classroom where there may be people who don't know each other. Yes, this may be a good thing to most. Me? I'm not positive at all, so of course it's going to be a bad thing. I hate school enough, so reliving a new part of it like at the beginning of the year makes me cringe. I'm reliving the memory of every classroom that I went into at the beginning of the year in my head. I don't want to be prone to mistakes like I did in every other classroom which now sticks with my reputation until the end of seventh grade and maybe even eighth. This is a new semester which means a new beginning.... Which will soon come to not a new or old ending but a same ending. A same ending as all the other ones. I'm thinking about all of this as I walk in and look around for a place to sit. I figure wherever I sit down I'll still want to be anywhere but here. I pick a random seat and try not to look around. I almost can't handle this, and I almost stand up to walk out of the classroom when the teacher starts to talk. "Hey guys and girls," he introduces himself. "I'm Mr. Taylor." I raise an eyebrow. Who the hell welcomes his classroom with hey guys and girls? Most teachers introduce themselves way more professionally. As I look at him though, he looked like he could have just graduated high school. He writes his name on the whiteboard with a bright green dry erase marker. He spells his name with handwriting almost as bad as mine. I expect him to go on and on about the rules of the classroom and such so when he turns around from the board I have to groan inwardly so no one can hear me. He turns around and smiles. "We're just going to get to know each other today." I'm so shocked that the inward groan comes outward. The outward groan sounds more like a deep squeak. All heads turn and eyes land on me. I instantly let my gaze drop. I don't know what to think about getting to know each other now. I'm thankful that Mr. Taylor isn't going to go through the rules. I would have felt restlessness in my legs and stretched my legs nonstop. I would be moving a lot. The meeting new people still does make me cringe. Now I wonder if it would be a good idea to try to start up a conversation. Yeah it probably would be another screw over but I'm too impatient for someone to come to me. I slowly raise my gaze. No one is looking at me. I could let out a sigh of relief, but I'm sure they must be thinking about me. Who can I start a conversation with? I don't see anyone, so I just stay put. Some late student walks into the classroom. She is the same girl I met at the beginning of sixth grade with the spiked hair and glasses. I remember at once at how I acted back then. She was there.

"I'm late," she says to Mr. Taylor in a voice that shows she doesn't even care. Mr. Taylor shrugs and when she turns around he shakes his head.

"Be right back class," he says. Before anyone can ask where he's out the door. It's obvious he needs to use the bathroom pronto. The girl who couldn't care less sits down two tables away from me. I try not to stare. I'm just about to look away when she sees me staring. She narrows her eyes into a glare.

"Julie!" She turns around at the voice of some kid in gothic clothes and I see the back of her sweatshirt. It says 666. The sign of the devil. My stomach churns in both disgust and disturbance. When she turns around she sees me still staring.

"What are you looking at BITCH," she snarls. I try to find words. The words I speak are a mistake.

"I was just reading your sweatshirt." A mistake. "YOU SLUT," she snarls louder. I feel like crying. I don't dare cry of course. I think of a comeback to say. "666, really?" A bigger mistake. Julie looks like she about to pounce on me. Luckily at that moment Mr. Taylor comes back into the classroom. Julie growls at me. It's so low that Mr. Taylor doesn't hear. I'm sure everyone else has. I drop my gaze again for the rest of the classroom period. When the bell rings I hurry out of the classroom. I push others aside because I'm so desperate to get away. When I do get away I go to in a corner in the school hallway and start to bawl.

I don't fully understand why other people cutting scares the shit out of me. I mean I do it, right? So why when I hear from my peers that a sixth grader has been cutting herself in the bathroom with scissors do I want to cry? So why when I come across a teenage TV show with a girl and her bloody wrists does it haunt me days on end after a just watch a small part of it? It doesn't make any sense. I don't like how it doesn't make sense. It's weird. When I'm in cutting mode, I don't think of any of this. How come? I don't know. If I'm cutting my mind is basically only focused on doing that. All in all, it just doesn't make sense. Now about cutting.... There can be multiple reasons why one cuts. The main common reason cutting happens is to get rid of the pain. That's the most obvious and expected reason. That's not all of it for me though. Yes, I cut when I'm in pain. Of course, I do that. That's the reason most of the times. There are other reasons though. I'll give two that can be combined together. Another reason is because I get angry. I get angry with everything around me. So, to take out that anger, I cut. I get so angry that I just cut. It's not a release of pain but a release of anger. Pretty horrific, right? Well, it gets worse. Yet another reason that I cut is to get attention. I want attention even if I'm getting it already. Add those together. Well, I can only imagine how that would be unsettling to others. That's what cutting does to me. It makes me someone I don't want to be. If it's out of pain, anger, or attention-seeking it makes me become someone I don't want to be. The worst part is adding other reasons beside pain. Nothing can get worse than this.

It so happens when I lose myself in my thoughts, I lose reality too. I get so caught up in my thoughts that I don't care about reality. I become someone that I'm usually not. I don't care about anything around me. This is especially true if I'm too deeply lost in my thoughts. When I'm like this I feel that everything bad is coming my way. I upset my family by this which upsets me even more. Today is a perfect case in point. I'm full of jealousy as usual when it comes to Megan and Ellie. They have a relationship I would die for. This is no joke. Their relationship is so close that it hurts me. I don't think they realize how much it does hurt me. If I confront Megan about this then she would be honest about it no matter what. If the honesty is the truth she never covers it up. Something I wish I could do also. Ellie would shrug it off like it would be no big deal. She would just keep going on like it didn't matter a huge amount. Again, something I wish I could do. They are talking in Megan's room and my thoughts become so negative I become selfish. I don't know this though because I'm so deep in my thoughts. I hurt a hurt that shouldn't be there. I don't know I'm causing my own hurt. I believe Megan and Ellie are doing this to me on purpose. I perceive everything about it this way even though it's not true. Everything turns on me and my sisters are targeting me, so they can hurt me. If I wasn't lost from reality I would know that this isn't true. Megan and Ellie wouldn't hurt me on purpose. Seeing their relationship and how I don't have that hurts, but it's not their fault. I don't always know that, unfortunately. There are facts that are true, however, that I know can't ever be changed. Megan and Ellie's relationship is something I can't change. I can't expect it to change by joining in on their relationship, even if there was a way to. I can't destroy the relationship they have in hope to start all over again, but with the three of us and not the two of them. No. It doesn't work that way. Their relationship is theirs only. They are still talking, so my feelings keep on getting on hurt and hurt. I have had enough. I march into Megan's room with a false smile stretched across my face. I don't know what I look like to them with the false smile, but right now I couldn't care less.

"Hi," I say. I don't know what their reaction is because I don't even notice. All of a sudden, I don't know what to say. I feel awkwardly stupid in front of my sisters which don't make much sense. I mean, they are my sisters. They have grown up with me. Most of all, they are my family. I don't have confidence around them really like I should. I spit out the words I mean to, but they take a different turn that I hoped.

"Why don't you include me? It isn't fair, and it hurts me so much!" They look at me and then at each other which sends a trail of fire down my spine, because seeing them even meet eyes makes me sick. I storm out of the room practically bawling. I realize I just made a huge deal. I hate myself for making such huge deals. I feel so awkwardly stupid still. I don't have any idea that only I felt this way. Not my sisters, but me. I can't figure out how to not be so full of envy. There's so much envy that I don't think of creating my own individual relationships with my sisters.

None of my other siblings attend Helena Middle School with me this seventh-grade year. Last year Danny was an eighth grader so now he's a freshman. Ellie was a fourth grader last year so now she's a fifth grader. Both of them are either two years ahead or two years behind me. Ellie will be here next year though as a sixth grader. By then I'll be an eighth grader. It's very uneasy being the only Volesky member in the school but I suppose if that's the way it's going to be, then that's the way it's going to be. No choice to stop but to go forward. At least I'm not alone on the car ride there. Well, obviously I'm not; because, I can't drive but still at least I'm not alone. My dad always drives me on the way to his work every morning of the week. Every morning since the first morning of my seventh-grade year in fact there's always this girl dressed in black walking down the side of the street. I always take interest in passing her for some weirdly unknown reason. The spot I always see her passing is by the railroad tracks. I point her out to my dad like I do every morning.

"Look dad," I say with great interest. "See there she is again!"

My dad nods. I turn to him with a big smile on my face. My dad focuses on driving. For the first time the realization comes into my head. I feel like I have to mention the girl in black every time I see her walking to wherever she is going with even the black color on her backpack. I feel like I have to, as a requirement if I want to get out of my dad's car to go into the school. If I don't say it, then I can't get out of the car. It's a must. I can't let it not happen. It doesn't make any sense at all. It's just something I have to do. Just like I have to say thank you to whoever drops me off at home or just like I have to say goodnight. Sometimes I have to say things over again and again if there is time. This is for the good night one. When I say goodnight and almost go to bed I forget that I have to brush my teeth or go to the bathroom or something. When I'm done doing what I forgot to do, I say goodnight again which I think is once more but instead is actually like three or four times more. When I'm satisfied I stop. The rare times when I'm not satisfied my parents have to help me through it. I'm glad my dad doesn't ever stop me from pointing out the girl dressed in black. I do have to say it every morning but repeating it in the short little time I have before reaching HMS? Well that would be hell for my dad. We stop at the stoplight because it's red and I watch the girl walk past us because she is going straight, and we have to turn. When we do turn she's already out of sight. My dad pulls up to the side of the road. I was obsessing about the girl dressed in black that I forgot I have to face another day of being the only Volesky family member at school. I shrug this off as I say goodbye to my dad. I go into the school with the thoughts of the girl dressed in black totally leaving my head.

The first person speaking is me just wanting answers. The second person is me just giving me unwanted answers....

"If there isn't hope then what is there?"

"Well that's a dumbass question. There is nothing."

"Then what can I do to find the hope I lost?"

"You seriously don't have an answer for that?"

"Well I wouldn't be asking if I did."

"You sure you want to know."

"Yes!"

"Alright you asked"

"Just tell me please!"

"The answer is simple: you can't find it."

"Okay if I can't find it what options do I have?"

"There are two. 1) Live without hope which is just like being dead 2) Die, die, and die." I'm not hearing voices in my head. These are just thoughts. All I'm doing is putting the thoughts out there, so it makes it easier to figure out. Even if it is a little easier it's still so much more than one can imagine. I have nothing to do so I'm focusing on what I'm lacking. I'm lacking hope. Hope is what one needs to survive. Hope is the ultimate feeling to have in order to go on. If one doesn't have hope, then what else is there? Well the answer is nothing except the people around who care, believe, and most of all love, and in the end, one must realize that that is the hope they needed. I may think that I have no hope, but my family is here surrounding me with support. The only time I won't have hope is for a couple years or so to come. That will be because I won't be on the right cocktail of medication and other reasons. It's all about the state of mind one can be in. If the chemical imbalance isn't treated correctly, then one won't even know what hope is. One will just lean toward doing anything to end whatever pain he or she is feeling. The pain then leads to the unthinkable. So, while I'm here saying out loud my thoughts, I hear the laughter of my little siblings. Jack and Nick must be coming home from the Broadwater Pool. I stand up and follow the laughter. Jack and Nick are downstairs watching TV now. I sit down on the couch and join them. They don't say a thing but just watch the show that's on. It's SpongeBob, a show I don't really care for. At that moment with their laughter still ringing pleasantly in my ears even though they really aren't laughing anymore makes whatever is on TV worth watching.

I go to class when the paranoia kicks on in full force. My pace picks up, but my class seems miles away. Out of the corner of my eyes I glance at the people around me. Three eighth graders are huddled in a corner. They are laughing. They are laughing at me. Did I do something wrong or embarrassing yesterday that I don't remember? Do I look funny today? Is there anything wrong with me in general? I pass an old sixth grade teacher of mine. She stops a student in the halls and starts talking to him. I bite back words that I want to say. It only takes me a minute to realize that I don't need to bite back any words. They won't come out anyway. No matter how hard I try they won't. It also only takes me a minute to realize that the words will never ever come out. I have no self-confidence. It's sad really, and it's no help at all. I pass more and more huddles of students and teachers talking to students. I even pass some parents walking through the halls. All the conversations are about me. I rush to my class now, but the conversations grow. I can't hear them clearly because there are so many of them. This is a good thing, but I can't even think about it. I can't think about anything good at all. When I reach class and it starts I have so much paranoia that I can't even pay attention to what my teacher is saying. I'm sure after class my teacher is going to talk to as many people as she can about how I didn't brush my hair and how my breath stinks. The paranoia keeps disrupting my attempts to try to understand what my teacher is saying. I try to focus, but it's no use.

The people around me can't wait to get out of class to talk about me. I debate whether to run out of class like I did last week and the week before and the week before that one. I'm so offended that everyone is talking about me. I do the hardest thing that I have been doing lately at least once a week, if not more. I get up and walk as fast as I can away from the class. I have been doing this so much and it never gets easier. It's the same and sometimes even harder. I go into the hall not even trying to calm my racing mind. I'm beyond that point. I sit down in the hall my face all red. When I run out of class it's not just because of the paranoia. If anything, else goes wrong it's the same result. Running out of class is always the same result. I'm very offended that everyone is talking about me. I am so offended that it makes me sick to my stomach and that's all it takes to make me want to barf on the spot.

Eighth grade: the last year of middle school. How did I get this far? It's a miracle really that I've made past the last hellish school years. Set one foot in front of the other and walk.... It should be as simple as that. Shouldn't it? Honestly no, it shouldn't. It shouldn't because I know better. I know better than to even believe in the word simple. It's not only the past hellish school years, but it's also the past hellish years with no school in it at all. I have lived through a nightmare with so much to overcome and I'm still living through a nightmare with so much to overcome. That's complicated not simple. I have realized that by now there is no simplicity. There is also nothing to look forward to. Yes, it's true that eighth grade is the last year at HMS.

That might be something to look forward to. It might be, but I'm not able to afford such happy thoughts. I'm a person that doesn't need, doesn't want, and doesn't have the ability to afford such happy thoughts. So, as I set one foot in front of the other, I remind myself that to go through school with simplicity is impossible for me. It's going through school with complexity that is possible for me. That's how I do it: even with no happy thoughts.

Ever since I was younger I was told to write down my feelings in a journal, so they don't explode in my brain. I never took this advice. I don't take the advice at all even now. I won't even write in my journal until I'm out of high school. I don't know why I choose not to do this when it's the advice from everyone who knows me and how much I struggle with my mental illness. It's like this with other things too: exercising daily, eating healthy, and regular sleeping schedule. I just don't do them. It's hard enough to live so why make the effort? I don't see what can come of it since life hurts so much at this point. I'm reminded of this because I'm going to see someone brand new that will probably tell me similar ideas. I'm sitting in the new, unfamiliar waiting room. I think that waiting rooms shouldn't be called this. Or at least for me. Waiting rooms make my palms sweat so badly that the sweat soaks through my pants and my nails get bitten to the point where they bleed. The worst part is the silence. It's so silent that it makes it clearer that no one wants to be here. I sure as hell am like that. This is the last place on earth that I want to be. My parents are beside me which should comfort me. It does the opposite. I'm so uncomforted. Them being here makes it worse, believe it or not! I feel like running out of here. I know better with my parents with me though. I slightly remember the first time I went to a therapist. I went there a few times back around the age of nine. Nell was about the same age as my parents. Possibly even older. I don't recall most of what we talked about. If there was one thing I recall somewhat clearly it was a toy doll in the waiting room. It had a poem on it about wanting to die. I read it every single time I went to the office. It freaked me out so much. It was to the point where I didn't even want to go to therapy. This was all because of some stupid doll. I hold my breath as I look around the waiting room. It's small, with music playing from a speaker in the ceiling. There are magazines of all sorts. There is a sign that reads: *We'll be there shortly.* My dad notices me reading the sign.

"What if it says we'll be there tall-ly," he jokes. I look up at him confused. My dad is being so bizarre. I read the sign again and shortly catches me eyes.

"Oh," I exclaim. "Short and tall! They're opposite!"

My mom nudges my dad and they smile. They have gotten my mind off of everything that I'm worrying about. Before I can be hurt that my dad tricked me, one of the doors of the waiting room opens. There she is. My new therapist, who I don't even know at all. My muscles stiffen, and fear swells up inside me. My parents stand up and I swear that's the only reason I can too. My new therapist directs the way into her therapy room. There are two rocking chairs and a couch. My parents sit on either side of me and I am soundless. I can't open my mouth to even introduce myself.

"I'm Marie." I don't meet my therapist's eyes even though I know her name now. I try to talk but my swelling fear has reached my throat. I'm speechless and I don't meet Marie's face. This is just great. For my whole therapy session, it's only my parents and Marie that talk. I just sit on the couch staring at my hands in my lap. I try to convince myself that I'm not even here. I'm trapped between my parents. My own freewill is trapped. I can't use my freewill to walk away. When the session ends Marie directs us back to the waiting room. My parents say goodbye and we walk to the car. The ride home is silent and for once silence feels right.

Gym is going to be outside today. I walk out behind my classmates, the last, as usual. My gym teacher is running late so one of the other gym teachers told us to wait outside. It's beautiful outside and I feel myself relax a little as I breathe in the nice fresh air. As usual, cliques form and I'm alone. I look up at the clouds seeing what shapes they form. This was a game I played with my siblings when I was younger. It was before things became so hard and so complicated. I missed being young where there was no worrying about anything or no wanting to kill myself. When I can't find any clouds that look like something in life I sigh and drop my gaze, disappointed. I click my tongue as I see how many cliques there` are. They are small cliques but there are so many. I start to shy away into the shadow of the bleachers when I see Laura and Javier talking. I have only seen Laura in the halls talking with girls like Polly and Gina. This should be a red flag to keep shying away to the bleachers, but I start heading over to her and Javier. Javier is the same Javier in sixth grade who mortified me when I threw up in class. This should be another red flag to keep away. This should be a double red flag even. I keep heading over. I think the reason why I head over is because they are the only people who aren't in a clique. Just like me. I can't be too sure the reason, unfortunately. I listen in to their conversation trying to be as casual as possible. "Yeah," Javier says. "What a pussy." I don't know how to join in the conversation, so I do it in one of the ways I normally do. I barge in.

"What's a pussy?" I ask as I step up to Laura's side. I'm thinking it's a cat, but the tone Javier was talking in makes me know he isn't talking about that. They both turn to me with their eyebrows raised. They look surprised but that changes at once. A smirk forms on Javier face and Laura struggles to keep laughter down her throat.

I suck my teeth in regret.

"Never mind," I mutter. I leave, Laura's laughter now leaving her throat. I'm still leaving when I hear Javier making fun of me to Laura. He is loud enough for me to hear. He does this on purpose of course.

"She doesn't know it's a vagina? Ha, ha, ha that's funny and lame at the same time." Laura stops laughing and quiets down. I realize that she doesn't think this is funny. She doesn't at all, but she doesn't have the guts to stand up for me. She probably doesn't want to, but it had to cross her mind since she stopped laughing right? Or at least something like that? My face burns and for the first time when my gym teacher shows up, I'm glad to go running.

Each time I go to Marie's, either my mom or dad come with me. This is because I can' open up. I'm as quiet as a rabbit. I'm able to look at Marie in the eye at least. That's some progress. It's getting hot outside as I walk up to the therapy building. If I stop and feel some metal post or something it would burn my hands. I wouldn't be able to put my hand there for more than five seconds unless I want it to get scorched. This shows how weather can change in Montana, just over the night. I'm roasting by the time I'm inside the therapy building. The air conditioning is too poor to make a difference. Just 15 steps from the car to here and my shirt sticks to me through my body sweat. My mouth yearns for water. Marie opens the door and my dad and my I go to the therapy room. It's such a short way from the waiting room that I could probably close my eyes to get here. I sit down on the now familiar couch with my dad. It's amazing how either my dad or Marie get impatient or frustrated with me because I barely talk. My mouth is sticky with saliva as Marie and my dad talk. I look at Marie as she asks me some questions again. I try to swallow but the saliva is too strong. Marie examines this. "Emma would you like a glass of water?" I talk without thinking.

"Yes, please!" The words come out with the sound of a disgusting smack. I instantaneously shut my mouth all embarrassed. Marie gets up and goes out the door. I avert my eyes from where she was sitting to the floor. My dad pats my back and I do my best not to cringe. Most of the time I'm the cuddliest, touchiest person you would ever meet. Under situations like this where I'm irritated at myself or someone else, I can barely stand being even in my own skin. It's my dad who is trying to comfort me, so I shouldn't cringe away. I try to deal with it, but I suddenly can't. I cringe, and he stops patting my back. I look up at him apologetically, but he just smiles understandingly. I'm glad he understands. If I were him, I would be totally offended by the cringe. Marie comes back and in her hand is a mug of water. She hands it to me which I take graciously. When I'm done drinking all of the water Marie smiles.

"Thank you," I say with a smile of my own. It's a small smile but still a smile, all the same. Marie stands up and so do my dad and me. The session is over already. I say goodbye to Marie for the first time that isn't just a wave. It's a smile, again only it's not so small.

I'm sitting in class when a girl I recognize around school comes in late. A substitute teacher taking my actual teacher's place while my teacher is on a sabbatical looks up from the poem she just started reading to us about irony. The girl hands the substitute teacher a green slip, who takes it trying not to look annoyed. She fails by a great extent. The girl takes a seat in the empty desk across from me. I try not to look but I can't help it. I recognize her, but I don't know where I have seen her before. The substitute teacher explains what irony is. I'm too busy still trying to figure out who this girl is. Quickly she turns to me. I expect her to glare or something, but she just smiles. I smile back. The bell rings and I go out of the class. The girl is going down the same hallway as me. I stop, and she stops. I turn to her.

"You look familiar," I blurt. What a way to start a conversation with someone I have never talked to before. She smiles to my surprise. Wow I didn't mess up for once.

"Yeah you look familiar too." I nod and smile back at her. She holds out a hand.

"I'm Annie." I shake it.

"And I'm Emma." We talk for a while trying to figure out where we have seen each other before. We can't figure it out, so we just think we just might have seen each other at the school. We leave it at that. I still find it weird that I can't figure out where I have seen her before. I mean, we both went to HMS for three whole years.

"Want to hang out sometime," Annie asks. Someone just asked me to hang out? Seriously?

"Yes!" We exchange numbers and I'm smiling for the rest of the day. I tell my parents later on about Annie after school. They are happy that I'm happy. When Annie and I talk on the phone later on that night we make plans to hang out this upcoming weekend. The weekend comes by slow but at least comes all the same. I go over to her house to spend the night. It's just Annie and her mom. She doesn't have a dad or any brothers or sisters. When I walk through her front door my nose wrinkles. It reeks of smoke. I try not to show how much this disgusts me. Annie gives me tour of her house having me thinking that this is so friendly of her. We take pictures, and she promises to give me copies. Later on, we drive to Shopko and get fake nails to glue onto our nails which later on I rip off leaving my real nails in unbelievable pain. The next day I go home feeling great. The Monday right after the weekend I feel that we can't be separated. The weekend and the weekends after that, Annie and I hang out nonstop. One weekend Annie says, "Emma, I can trust you so thank you." I feel the same. I can trust Annie and that's what matters. One night after the town spring carnival, Annie looks up at me.

"You know what, Emma? Wouldn't it be amazing if you got your ears double pierced like mine?" I nod hastily.

"Yes, that would be amazing!" I think she's going to take me to get my ear pierced when she pats the pillow.

"Here lay down." I blink in confusion but do as I'm told. "Okay I'll get some ice. I'm going to numb your ear, so you won't feel the needle in your ear too much." I swallow as I realize what's happening. I don't want to do this. I don't want to do this. I don't want to do this. I don't speak up. The reason that stands out the most is that she trusts me. Whatever happens she still needs to trust me. I can't ruin her trust no matter what. When she comes back with the ice in a bowl and a silver needle I force a painful smile on my face to hide me fear. "Ready?" I give her a thumbs up regretfully. She sits down beside me and does the first ear. I swallow down at the agony it gives me. The next ear gives me the same amount of agony, if not more. The whole time the word *trust* repeats in my head again and again and again. When it's over I begin to worry that the piercings in my ears are uneven. I immediately ask for a mirror. She hands me her hand mirror and I look. I can't tell if the piercings are even or not. I almost ask Annie if they are but the word trust repeats in my head some more. Annie then starts talking about the football game that's going on tonight. It's crosstown. I momentarily forget about the piercings. Annie takes me by the hand and pulls me toward the kitchen. On the counter is the hair dye she bought for me when we went shopping. I get excited.

"We're gonna dye my hair now?!" Annie smiles wide.

"Yes, Emma, of course we are!" Annie helps me get my whole head wet in the sink and the she starts putting the dye in my hair. When she's done she tells me I can't move my head for about twenty minutes. I tense. I can barely hold still for even thirty seconds. I have to be doing something. I hold as still as I can. After what feels like centuries of fighting to stay still, I can finally move. I stretch my head to the mirror and admire my newly colored hair. It's a lighter brown with a tint of a plumb color to it. I like it a lot. We go to the front door to walk to the middle school for the crosstown game. Annie's house is right between Helena High School and Helena Middle School, so we can walk to either building easily. They aren't even a mile and a half apart. Crosstown means that the two local schools are playing together. Helena High School (HHS) and Capital High School (CHS) are rivals. The rival is so intense because HHS hasn't won a championship since the 1930's. CHS always wins. They make sure they are known as the best school with the best sports. They use their sport status as an excuse to dominate anyone who dares to go against them. Of course, each year a fair amount of HHS students still believe we can win. I applaud them for that. I place my hand on the Annie's doorknob all pumped up with excitement about the game. Even though HHS probably won't win I have to be there to support them. Besides I'm proud that next year I'm going to be a Bengal. I'm about to turn the doorknob when I remind myself that this isn't my house. I quickly take my hand away. Annie laughs, and relief overfills me. Annie takes out her cell phone.

"We have a lot of time," she says slowly. Disappointment covers the features of excitement on my face.

"How much time?" A grin forms on Annie's face.

"Enough to finish my great idea!" She goes to the kitchen and returns with scissors. I stare at the scissors with deep shock.

"I think we should trim your hair!!!!"

"Huh?" She nods happily.

"Don't worry Emma I'm good at this." I hesitate for a moment, but the word trust starts repeating in my head again. I take a deep breath in and force a smile on my face.

"Sure." My sure is so false that I half pray that Annie recognizes it and will put a stop to this. This doesn't happen. I think of my parents at once and have a pretty good idea of what they will say about my ears and now what's going to be my soon trimmed and dyed hair. We go out to the porch and she starts to cut. I squeeze my eyes shut. I'm filled with so much regret that I don't notice how still I am.

"There," Annie announces when she's done. "You look fantastic girl!" I laugh a fake laugh. Annie's too proud of herself to notice how fake it is. She hands me a hand mirror. I hold it away stupidly.

"Look at yourself! You're so pretty!" I slowly raise the hand mirror to my face and study my reflection. It doesn't look all that bad to my surprise. As I look down at my feet though my mouth drops open. A lot of what was my hair is on the ground.

"Yeah, you had a lot of hair. This is still a trim though. I promise. If I cut an inch more than it would be a cut." I shut my mouth. She trusts me, so I need remember that and keep it in my mind. "Guess what else I'm gonna do?" I swallow hard. What in the world could be next? I answer knowing very well that my voice is shaky.

"W-what?"

"I'm going to take you to the game now. Ready?" Most of my worries fade away as excitement pumps me up again.

"I'm ready more than ever!" As we walk to the game my anxiety goes up. Even with my friend Annie I can't help but feel that everyone is watching my every move, waiting for me to make a fool out of myself. I can hear the hollers of people at the game already even though I'm three blocks away. I take a deep breath and try to appear as natural as I can next to Annie. I hope she doesn't notice. When we reach the gate, I dig out my ticket from my pocket and hand it to the lady. After Annie does the same the lady waves us through. The hollering is at its highest peak now and it takes all my willpower not to back away to go out the gate. Annie leads the way to the stands. I keep up, with my heartbeat pounding so hard in my chest it feels like it's about to explode, and my mind racing so much with thoughts that I can't keep up with even one of them. The Bengals play the nearest toward the HMS building and the Bruins play by the gate which keeps the field and road separated. When we reach the stands, Annie stops and lets out an exasperating sigh. "Of course," she mutters. "Of course, the stands are for the high school students and the high school students only." I get what she means as I look up and see only older teenagers standing in the stands portraying all their high and mightiness. I don't scowl like Annie does. I don't have the guts to.

"Let's get something to eat." Before I can agree, Annie is already going to buy food. I rush to keep up with her. When we reach the snack stands I see how long the lines are. People are all around me which if course isn't all that good for me. The longer Annie and I wait in line, the harder it is for me to keep my mind calm. Each time a person gets out of line and Annie steps up to close the gap ahead of us, I have to urge myself forward with all my might. I almost topple over Annie from taking a huge step because of the urging. I want to go home, but I don't want to disappoint Annie. She is my only friend and I don't want to lose her. Deciding whether to stay or go is like a war in my head. The longer the war goes on, the harder it is to decide. I get so worked up it's like a bomb is going to go off any second. I decide when we finally get toward the front of the line with only two people ahead of us.

"I have to go home Annie." Annie turns to me, but I don't see even a hint of disappointment on her face. Instead her face is full of concern.

"Are you okay," she asks.

"I'm just a little tired that's all," I lie. Annie smiles and I smile back. I walk away wishing I didn't have such issues. I walk toward the gate where there are less people. It's only when my mom picks me up that I remember my newly pierced ears and hair trim. I ignore the regret within me. When my mom meets me at the curb of the street, I take a deep breath. I'm so shaken up that I don't want to deal with anything. My mom doesn't say anything on the way home and for this I'm grateful. The next weekend I see something I never saw before. My mom drops me off at Annie's grandpa's gas station. I wave goodbye to my mom and go to the back where Annie was.

"Annie, hey!" I go up to give her a hug when I see she's staring at the counter where her arms are resting. I walk over uncertainly. She is shaking a bit which scares me.

"Annie?" She looks over and I see tears in her eyes. I rush over but stop at once when I see a knife on the counter by her arms. My eyes stare at the knife and then I take in what I see next. Her arms are full of scars. There are scars that are healed over and there are scars that are fresh. The healed scars are lines going all the way up and down her arms. The new scars are fresh with blood. I start to tremble as I realize that Annie cut herself with the knife on the table. I've seen cut wrists, but not arms. Not as many as I see now. Annie starts to bawl, and I unexpectedly overcome my shock and hold her as her bawling becomes more and more uncontrollable. "It's okay," I comfort her. "It's going to be okay?" We stay there for what feels like forever. I still tremble but thankfully Annie doesn't notice. Her trembling mixes with mine. Later on, in the evening we go get our nails done. The lady who is doing our nails sees Annie's arms and her eyes go wide.

"Honey," she says carefully. "What happened to your arms?" Annie's stuck on how to answer so I answer for her. With a lie that is.

"Her cat scratched her." The lady has a look on that makes it obvious that she disbelieves.

"Right." She doesn't ask about it anymore. After both of our nails are done we go back to her house.

"Thank you," she says gratefully. I nod but feel guilty for lying. Later on, that night Annie has a hard time again. I see on a piece of paper that she wrote something about Laura. It says that she is a bitch. I feel uneasy again and wonder when she hung out with Laura. I feel Annie's eyes on me and quickly take my gaze off the paper. At that moment Annie starts to bawl again. I feel exhausted as I have to hug and comfort her again. Suddenly Annie breaks away and grabs her home phone. I don't know whose number she is dialing but I bet its Laura's. Annie leaves a message telling Laura how much she hurt her. She also drops the F bomb a couple of times which made me cringe. When she disconnects the phone, she starts to bawl again. This is just too tiring. I hug and comfort her yet again. Later on, Annie tells me that it was Laura's home phone she left the message on. I swallow stunned that Annie could actually do that. I want to make her feel better. I can't think of anything, but then I remember the piece of paper. I go over to the paper and write that Laura is the biggest bitch ever. I feel like a disgusting person. I would do anything to make Annie feel better though. She trusts me, so it's worth it. Also, when she always does my makeup and hair perfectly I feel like I should do anything to make Annie feel better. It's the least I can do, besides what I have been doing at the moment. The next day I'm missing my favorite designer sweats. I look all over my house for them. It's only later on that Monday that I see Annie wearing them. I don't know

166

what to feel or what to think. She could have asked me to borrow them. The fact that later on I see her talking to Polly who is complimenting her on them, and she doesn't even say they are mine hurts me. That was that for me. I can't be her friend anymore. When she doesn't even contact me anymore I start to believe that the whole trust thing was a waste. What I can't be sure of is, if I was the one who ended a great friendship or not.

If there is a point in life of forgiveness I don't know it. I'm not talking about not knowing how to forgive others. No, that's easy. I forgive easier than I forget. I'm talking about forgiving myself. I don't forgive myself. Hell, I can't forgive myself. It's not only uneasy. It's impossible. I hope that one day that there will be a possibility to forgive myself. Is it my fault or my mental illness? It's too hard to know. I punish myself in a lot of ways. I cuss and scream and shout inside my horrible thinking mind. I don't let my tears out so my head aches crazily. I blame the worst things on my conscious. I don't even have the courage to blame my mental illness. Today an intrusive thought enters my already twisted tangled string of thoughts. Go away, go away, and go away. I plead this so much. I have had a lot of intrusive thoughts before. It mostly just involves the passing thought of mutilating my siblings. They pass, not stay. There can be triggers for the intrusive thoughts, obviously. Other times it just comes randomly. Both scare me, but somehow it coming randomly scares me more. Today this intrusive thought is the first one that doesn't pass and is random. I'm with my siblings when all of a sudden, I think of grabbing a hammer and smashing it into one of their skulls. Go away, go away, and go away. I get up and rush upstairs. I end up lying on the smaller couch in the living room, rather than my bed in my room. It's like I can't breathe. I close my eyes using all of my strength to force the thought gone. I don't have much strength. It swallows me whole until I really can't breathe. It's not until later on that I realize that I'm the one holding my breath and not my mental illness. What feels like hours later my mom comes into the living room? Finally, someone has found me. Wait a minute. Do I really want to be found after this horrible incident? I put my face in the cushion. My mom comes to me and pulls me up. "Emma? What's wrong?" I want to tell her. I want to tell her so badly. It's eating me up until there's no point of redemption left. I open my mouth to tell her then shut it then open it then shut it. I'm struggling here. My mom has other things to deal with. She must think that if I'm not going to tell her then it's not very important. She must think that, but she doesn't know. She doesn't know that I'm unable to tell her, just like everyone else. She gets up and I let out a wail. She turns to me. I need to get it out. With the very little strength I have left I tell her what I'm thinking. She listens wholeheartedly but it still hurts a lot to know that she and no one else will totally understand me. She tells me to do something else to distract myself. If that doesn't help, then go to sleep and everything will be better tomorrow. This is something she and my dad tell me to do. It's also something my therapist Marie tells me to do. I decide to go straight to sleep. I don't have anything to hope for except wishing for no tomorrow. I lay in my bed tossing and turning. I finally get rid of the intrusive thought by changing it with the whole thought of not knowing how to forgive myself. When I fall asleep I dream of forgiving myself only to completely forget about all of it in the morning.

I'm in math: the hardest subject that I'll ever have to learn which in result, will make me eventually forget everything after middle school and also high school. I stare at my paper, tears filling my eyes. This is too frustrating. My brain can't take in the fractions and decimals. They blur into a mix right in front of my vision. All of these numbers don't make sense. They tumble over each other making it into a bigger mess. No, I'm not hallucinating. I'm just giving an idea at how hard math is to me. It's excruciatingly hard. Not only am I aware of that. I'm also aware of the fact that everyone around me might as well be gaping at the girl just crying over her paper. I can't take it. There's too much pressure. Way too much pressure. I want to take the paper and rip it into a trillion of pieces. I won't do that though. I'll be seen as an even crazier person. So instead I get up and run out of the classroom. Just like I started in fifth grade and ever since then I have been doing it; running away. I wait in the hall my head between my knees. This isn't a new thing in my eighth-grade math class. It's at least once a week. Yes, it's that hard for me. My math teacher, Miss Lowry, immediately follows me into the hall yet again. "Emma," she says. She's trying to understand. That means so much. Her brother committed suicide right before she started her teaching job in Dillon.

I don't look up between my knees. I'm too horrified, too mortified. Miss Lowry crouches down next to me.

"You can't keep doing this," she says in a soft voice. I still don't look up. My tears are hot now. They are leaving trails of fire on my face unable to cool down. I don't want them to cool down. I need them as a reminder of how useless I am as a person. I'm fully alert that Miss Lowry needs to get back to her class. She left them alone just to check on me.

"You can't keep doing this," she repeats. "If this happens again, then I have no choice to give you a referral." I nearly stop breathing. It sounds more like if this happens again then I have no choice to *punish* you with a referral. I get up on wobbly knees and follow Miss Lowry back into class. She walks me to my seat. She actually walks me to my seat. It's not like I'm a child so why does she do this? Why does she do this right in front of everyone? She goes back to her desk and I stare at the paper. Now I stare at the paper not even noticing the fractions and decimals. Actually, I don't notice anything because I'm staring at the paper so hard willing my mind to disappear.

I have always wanted to be in a situation where I can show my younger siblings that I can protect them just as much as Megan and Danny can. Oh, and no this isn't something I want to make a competition out of. I swear it isn't. This is out of care and compassion. Ellie is a sixth grader here. She attends HMS just like me and it's only me and her here. What does this give? This gives a chance that I can show her that I can protect her. If I show this, she can look up to me more. She can tell Paul, Jack, and Nick that I, even with my mental illness, am capable of protecting them, too. I may not be able to protect them a lot, but I can do my best. Ellie has friends that she hangs out with, so I need to make sure she has that time. What I learned at the beginning of the year is that Ellie needs time with her friends. I have also learned that Ellie likes to hang out with her friends without being interrupted. What I mean by this is that she doesn't want me to be around her and her friends. This should be expected. Ellie is experiencing a whole new school with whole new friends. Why should she be interrupted? Shouldn't she have this opportunity? I mean, after all, it really is a new experience. She deserves this new experience and a good one at that. I don't want her to have my horrible experience of paranoia and anxiety that happened even before the official first day of school. She seems happy and she should be happy. Of course, there's something else that should be expected. This has to do with me. I have a lot of feelings seeing how happy Ellie is. I have a feeling of wanting Ellie to stay happy. I have a feeling of wanting Ellie not to be interrupted by me, so she won't have to worry about being happy. I have a feeling of wanting Ellie to convince me that I don't need to constantly check on her to see if she's happy, even if I can't convince myself. There are also the feelings of selfishness and jealousy of seeing how happy Ellie is. I have a feeling of wanting the friends, laughter, and smiles, as well as the hugs they exchange with Ellie. I have a feeling of wanting to have the outgoingness, the happiness, the everything else-ness Ellie has. I have a feeling of wanting to try out the experience so much. I don't and won't ever have this opportunity of course. I don't know what's more powerful to me. I want happiness for Ellie, but I also want happiness for me. Ellie needs time, so I try to stay away from her. One day she passes me in the hall. I'm having a bad day, and I need someone to talk to. I smile painfully, and she can tell something's wrong. I expect her to keep walking, but she doesn't. She stops and waves me over to her. I should be cautious or at least hesitate before going over. I should think it over. I don't, though. As usual, I act on instinct. I'm having a bad day so that should be reasonable. Sadly, this last thought doesn't even cross my head. I go over to her with tears in my eyes. Before I can tell her what's wrong the bell rings. Ellie gives my arm a quick squeeze. "I'm here ya know," she says before leaving me for her art class. This should comfort me, but it doesn't. In fact, it makes things worse. I need her now. She's here for me and I need her now. As I run past people to get to Ellie, it doesn't register in my mind that she's going to be the one who needs protection a lot in the future. I'm also going to be the one that's going to need protection in the future. I'm the one who will need most of the protection from my older siblings and sometimes even my younger siblings. Ellie is in shock when I nearly run her over. Her gaze isn't focused on me. Her gaze is on her friends. Ellie feels helpless in this situation where I think I'm the only helpless one.

"I'm having a really terrible day," I sob. "I don't know what to do!!!" Ellie stands still but only for a second. It's only when she tears away from me that I realize that I was gripping her shirt.

"Go to class," she begs. "Go to class Emma. The bell rang. Just go to class." I take a step back and blink. I turn around and swallow. Everyone's watching this. Oh shit. What had I just done?

"Yeah," I say. "Yeah I'll go to class." I turn to leave but not before I see Ellie glare at me. I'm disgusted with myself. I'm so disgusted with myself. I always mess people's lives up. This is what I do for a living. I don't mean to ruin lives but can there even be an excuse in this situation? I reach my next class feeling miserable. It's even harder to focus today. Well this is obvious, but I'm in a darker place than I usual. When I get to class, I can't focus. I feel the urge to grab the pen on the desk next to me and stab myself in the chest or something. I want to drink the ink, so I can get poison or something. I want to...

"Emma?" I look up and see my English teacher looking at me. I look down at the article the class is reading. It's my turn to read. I quickly take a risky random guess where I am. I read out loud messing up on a lot of words. Luckily, I end up reading the right paragraph. Not so luckily that when I'm done reading the paragraph that I keep eyeing the pen. I want it bad. I want it so, so, so, so bad. When the bell rings it hits me that I'm the one who needs the protection. I need it from my older siblings, but do I really need it from my younger siblings too? Poor Ellie, poor, poor, poor, poor Ellie. I don't know until this day, that out of my whole family, I'm going to be the one who needs protection the most, and that's a true sign of weakness right there. How pathetic can I get? Probably more than this, which isn't so hard to believe. Screw it all. I just want that pen.

I'm sitting outside of the circle of my classmates who are sitting on the grass. I'm waiting for my ride as I listen in to Mikey who is leading the conversation. Okay I'm eavesdropping but I'm so bored waiting for my ride. Mikey is telling everyone about some guy who is mentally handicapped. Or rather making fun of the guy who is mentally handicapped. This sickens me. How can people be so cruel? I grind my teeth together when everyone in the group is laughing by now. It's only when Mikey starts talking about the guy being nuts in the head because he has to take psychotic pills that have side effects like weight gain and shakiness, that I'm about to burst. I start to walk to them when I suddenly grasp what is really going on here. Mikey has it wrong. He's actually talking about the guy dealing with being mentally ill and not dealing with being mentally handicapped. I hold my breath, my anger turning into devastation. I have to correct him. I just have to. I walk the rest of the way over, trying to gain courage and confidence. It's hard to though, with all the pain that's piercing me from the inside out from hearing the story Mikey is telling everyone. They all look up at me and I feel like prey. I ball up my fists to try to seem fiercely brave. Unfortunately, when I speak my small voice make my balled fists look out of place.

"Mikey," I say. "Um, you're, uh, wrong...." Mikey looks shocked that I have even come up to him to speak, let alone say that he's wrong. Of course, the shocked look turns into a deceitful smirk.

"How am I wrong?" I clear my throat which sounds out of place here with everyone staring at me.

"You're saying that the guy was mentally handicapped. That's not right. That's actually where you're wrong. He's mentally ill, and what you're saying is not very nice. In fact, it's not nice at all. It's just plain mean." Mikey's deceitful smirk turns downward making his face look awfully twisted.

"No. You have it wrong of course. Being mentally handicapped is the same as being mentally ill." I shake my head, but this is a horrible mistake even though the headshake isn't directed at anything expect the mean nature that Mikey is cursed with. Mikey laughs meanly. "Shaking your head won't change a thing." He gives me the evil eyes. "And there's another name for both of them that categorizes them together. Do you know what that is?" I don't answer. Hell, he doesn't give me time to answer even if I wanted to. His voice turns menacing as he answers his own question. "Mental retardation." My face turns red and my eyes start to fill up with tears. I turn on my heel and run away. If only I had the ability to stand up for myself, to humiliate Mikey like he just did to me. It would be such a sight to see him run off instead. To see him cry would be the best. I run around the school looking like a freak. I only do this because I have to reach the spot where my ride is going to pick me up without passing Mikey in the group. If only I could be stronger.

Battling my mental illness for some freedom gets so hard that I don't really battle at all. I'm defeated within seconds. That's basically my life: battling mental illness to no end. It never stops. It's a war that will last through all my life. I don't even know where to start to try to win the war. Part of me probably doesn't even want to start. That part doesn't want to try because it actually believes there IS no way to win. Soon that part becomes the whole part and every cell in my body believes it. I'm a failure in defeating my mental illness. That is that. How do I survive? Well that's a hard one to answer. It seems like I don't survive it. I mean I'm here. I'm here doing day-to-day things. I do walk. I do talk. I do eat. I do drink. I do sleep. I do most things. I'm here. I'm totally here. I'm here but.... But that's just how everyone else views it. I view it completely differently though. I may be here but what people don't know is I almost can't bear it. I suffer everyday always wanting to die. Imagine not being able to function because knives are floating around the air and the want to grab onto one is so powerful, it's all one can do to try to ignore it. Imagine not being able to stay in school, so running out seems like the only option, and the want to run outside the school's parking lot into the road to get hit by a car is so tempting, that one practically prays for that to happen. Imagine not being able to have any friends at all and wanting them so bad that one will be humiliated a million times without a care, just to experience friendship, even knowing it's a 95% chance that the friends aren't true. Imagine all of these, plus everything you can think of that will destroy one's life, whether it would be slitting skin, so it burns like hell or picking scabs, so it hurts like hell. Imagine all the pain in the world balled up and thrown at your face. Imagine to only feel all of this with, while at the same time being numb, so as to feel nothing at all. No this isn't an exaggeration. This is the reality of me and probably others suffering with mental illness. The only way out of this agonizing pain, this never-ending pain, is to kill oneself. This is why I'm always being defeated by the war of mental illness. There is just no chance of defeating it. Even if I seem like I'm here I'm also somewhere else: an unbearable hell.

I crawl in bed in tears. I just came back from church. I hate church because it's so boring and I can't keep up with the readings. I don't even know what half of the words in the bible means when the readings are being read. I feel guilty because of this. I'm a Catholic. I'm a freaking Catholic. My parents do their best not to miss a Sunday. My mom's the youth minister at the biggest church in Helena: The Cathedral. This isn't why I'm crying though. I'm crying because when I'm church I think about things that aren't supposed to be thought about in church: having sex, doing drugs, drinking alcohol, cussing silently, wanting death. I even hate God. This isn't the main reason why I'm crying though. What's the main reason I'm crying? I'm crying because I want to know why. Why was I given these terrifying mental illnesses? Why do I have to deal with them? Why couldn't it be someone else? Why do I feel so alone? Why can't anyone understand? Why, why, why, why? WHY ME? I wonder if I did something wrong to deserve this. My parents say I was born with this because we have a history of it in the family so how did I do something to deserve this? It doesn't make sense. I feel like somehow this is my fault. Is it though? I'm so confused. WHYYYYYYYYYYYYYYYY?!!!!! I don't know. I don't know. All I know is that I want to go away, so I do something I haven't done on my own for a while. I pray:

"God, please take me away. I don't deserve to be here. I don't want to be here. Take me away in my sleep while I take a nap. I can't handle this pain. It's hard feeling it. I can barely handle this. Take me away so I don't kill myself and go to hell. I'm scared of going to hell, but I don't know how much longer I can hold onto the word called "life". Please, please, please take me away. Amen.

P.S. If you don't do it during my nap then tonight is okay too. Just no later than that. Thank you."

I fall asleep right then holding onto that prayer as much as I can. What I don't realize is that I'm holding onto something so much tighter. I'm holding onto that word called "life." <3

Writing.... I was told ever since I can remember how good I am at writing. Since the first computer we owned back in the late 1990's with one of the oldest Microsoft Word programs, I would write. I can't remember to this day the first story I wrote as a child in elementary school. The way my dad was stunned and always praised me for my writing made me feel special. It wasn't until later on in my high school years that I realized how true it was. It wasn't until later on in my high school years that I realized this was most likely a talent I got from having mental illness. I hated that at first, but over the years I didn't mind it so much. I didn't like where it came from, but it still gave me something to do. The thing is, no matter how far I get in a story, I always ending up deleting it because I'm never satisfied. Never ever, ever, ever. I started writing poems in middle school. On this last day of eighth grade I relax a lot. It's right at that day, that hour, that moment that as I think about eighth grade ending I start to write like a maniac:

If there's an end it's today.
It's the end of a long painful parade.
I feel so bonkers about leaving.
I'm so excited there's no grieving.
There's no time for anything but smiles.
I could run and run for miles.
Ha, ha, ha just kidding but still.
There are no more tests to show weak skills.
Any weakness remaining is gone in a flash.
There is no worry about acting rash.
I'm fine for lake time and summer.
Hey that's not a bummer.
If there's an end it's today.
It's the end of a long painful parade.

I look at this poem in surprise satisfaction. Of course, I feel it's not the best, which makes me almost rip it out. I'm seriously close to it. What distracts me from that is an idea for another poem.

Take me away take me away
I don't want to sway
Finding answers isn't easy at all
It makes me want to fall
I'm over everything that made me cry
This is a fib and I don't know why
I'm worried for next year
I swear I'll try not to shed a tear
The day is wavering to be over
Soon it'll be as lucky as a four-leafed clover
I need to stop thinking negatively
I need to use some creativity
Take me away take me away
I don't want to sway

I compare both the poems. They aren't perfect. They aren't good. I sigh and crumple the papers up. I throw them in a nearby garbage can when the bell rings as a reminder for everyone to pick up their yearbooks in their fourth period class. I go grab my yearbook and wait on the road behind HMS. Both my parents pick me up and I remember one similarity from both the poems: they both lie. It's not the end and I do want to sway.

PART - 4

Tightly wound up in my own prison. I don't know why I feel like this. It's been a good day. I mean I just got home from camping. It was beautiful camping. The river was nice and warm. It was also calming in a way. The way it passed me with its sound of trickling. It was almost like a soft murmur telling me to let go of my worries and enjoy myself. The gentle breeze that shook the pine trees a bit. That sound calmed me too. It also was almost like a soft murmur telling me the same thing as the river. The surprising thing was that I did let go of my worries and I did enjoy myself. So why now do I feel suffocated?

Legendary Lodge: the place where I could live forever if I could. It's a Catholic camp for the grades 5-12. I have gone to Legendary for all the years except for one. It was the seventh-grade camp that I couldn't attend because it was canceled due to the fire warnings. I was so sad because my suitcases were all packed and I was ready to go. Luckily, I didn't stay sad for long because that meant I could have more computer time which I spent most of my time on in the summer with there being nothing else much to do. The rest of the years I went of course. I wouldn't ever miss it. Legendary Lodge is the one and only place where I can feel at peace with God. I'm without much worry really. The lodges are on an island. To get to the island you have to take a boat, of course. It's so much fun riding the boat even if it's only a minute or two ride or even less. It's the summer before freshman year. My nerves are up as usual. They don't change even if I do things over and over again. I sit in the boat trying not to shake. Across the lake I see the camp counselors screaming welcoming greetings and waving their hands everywhere. I want to drop to the bottom of the boat so I'm out of sight. I don't know why I'm unsettled because of them doing this. It just makes me feel out of place or something. Maybe it's a mixture of excitement and nervousness. Heck, I don't know. I get off the boat with my suitcase. I grip the handle to stop my shaking. It doesn't help and I'm again aware of how out of place I feel. I bite my bottom lip trying not to give into the urge to turn back around and go home, even if I have to swim across. My older brother Danny is behind me and nudges me forward gently. I relax quite a bit. Danny drove all the way up here with me. He took the time away from his friends and girlfriend to spend the hour ride with me and to make sure I'll get settled in easily. I walk through the camp and breathe in the fresh air I haven't breathed in since last summer. I can't even try to imagine what it would be like not being able to come to camp as a camper here after the summer before senior year. I go to the main cabin to check in. The camp counselors give me a nametag made out of tree bark and tell me which cabin that I'll be staying in. The next thing I have to do is check in my meds. Yes, it's in another check in area so it's not where anyone can see but it still makes me embarrassed. At once I'm bitter, and the paranoia comes onto me in overload. I walk up and take my pill box out of my bag. I place them onto the table. The camp counselor is a cute guy. I don't meet his eyes completely.

"Do you want to keep this in your cabin?"

I now meet his eyes completely. "Huh?"

My response sounds stupid, and I bite my tongue way too hard. The skin from my tongue goes down my throat and I do my best not to gag at the sickening texture. Blood overfills my mouth. The thought of my swallowing skin makes me wonder if I'm a cannibal. I have to remind myself that Marie says that I'm not. As I swallow the blood the camp counselor explains to me what he means.

"You can take the pills to your cabin now. You're going to be in high school. Am I wrong?" My response is quick, so I don't slur on my blood. If I slur he'll think I'm drunk, or worse, crazy. Not that the latter isn't too far off. He smiles, which sadly doesn't make me any less tense.

"Thanks." I hurry and grab my suitcase, my thoughts on the run. Danny doesn't say a thing, for which I am grateful. I don't know if he even noticed how I was feeling but I am still grateful. He stops outside of my cabin.

"You all set?" he asks.

"Sure," I say. What kinds of response is this? He gives me a hug which does make me less tense.

"Remember," he says. "Just have fun!" I nod in hope that his words will stay with me during this whole week at Legendary Lodge.

"Bye, Emma! I love you!"

I smile broadly. "Bye, Danny. And I love you too."

He turns his back and heads to the dock to get a ride back across the lake while I turn my back and go into my cabin. Some of the bunk beds are taken. Where do I go? Will I disrupt someone if they want a bunk I want? Would that be a bad thing? I choose a top bunk in the corner of the cabin. I take my sleeping bag and unroll it onto the top bunk's mattress. I sit on the top bunk swinging my legs back and forth as girls come in and out of the cabin. I do this until a girl comes in looking for a place to set down her suitcase. I force a smile on my face as she comes toward me. She places her suitcase on the bottom bunk.

"Hi."

She looks up at me shyly. "Oh, hi."

My smile isn't all that forced anymore.

"I'm Emma." I extend out my arm, so she can shake my hand. She's short like me too.

"I'm Tess."

Her voice is soft. She's so shy I can barely hear her voice. She takes my hand and shakes it. I'm cautious not to shake too hard. I'm never ever cautious. I usually do whatever I want. In other words, I try to push myself out of my comfort zone. I push myself a little too hard most of the time. I do things that make the atmosphere awkward and weird. It's hard to explain, to get a full concept of how it truly affects the person or people around me. Tess sits on the bottom bunk and it's silent again. I remind myself that I'm doing well. I can't screw things up too badly. Or at least I can try not to. The bell rings signaling dinner. We go leave and I clear my throat.

"Have you been here before?"

She nods. "Yeah, only twice."

I nod waiting for her to say more. She doesn't. I debate what to say next. I don't want to mess up a new friendship.

"Where are you from?"

"Bozeman."

I nod now. She doesn't say more again and I'm disappointed. Worries that I messed up fill my head.

"And you?" Finally, she speaks.

"Helena."

She tilts her head to the side. "That's neat."

I just shrug. "Yes, I guess."

She laughs and I'm shocked.

"Yeah, I guess that is how to describe Bozeman too."

She just lets out a laugh. This makes me happy and I beam. We reach the main cabin and go into the room where food is served. I sit down and wait for Tess to sit down beside me. When she doesn't sit down I look up. She's walking to another table. I'm about to stand up and follow her when she sits down by a person who she does most likely know. I feel like I just got smacked in the face. She did say she has been here twice before so why should I assume she didn't know anyone else? Her shyness maybe just gave me that impression. The table I'm sitting at fills up quickly. I try to be casual. I don't want any disappointment visible on my face. I know a few people around me from the last few summers or so ago. The few people are girls: Shellie and Alice. I'm surprised not to see the other two girls that weren't there: Vivian and Jo. The words that vibe off of them when all four are together: WE WILL COME TO YOU TO BE YOUR FRIEND IF WE WANT. Last summer I ignored the worded vibe. Shellie and Alice are the two who really bug me when they are together. They sit by me and talk about stuff at home. I do my best not to grimace. We're at Legendary Lodge not home. We're here for God and Jesus. We're here for our faith which we can take home afterwards. I close my eyes when Alice takes her cell phone out of her pocket. It isn't allowed to bring cell phones. This just ticks me off. When I open my eyes I'm glad her cell phone is back in her pocket. The food comes around and I do my best to eat nicely. My eating habits can be disgusting because I eat so fast. After everyone is done eating, we go out to do evening activities like Fruit Basket Upset. I cheat of course by scooting over a couple of spots instead of running across the circle. I don't want to be the only one standing. I couldn't stand doing that. That night I lay in bed thinking about what may happen until Friday. The next few days (Monday, Tuesday, and Wednesday) I become somewhat more comfortable and I don't shake at all. Mass happens once a day for about half an hour. Sometimes it's in the afternoon, sometimes it's in the evening, and sometimes it's even at night. There are activities to do which I like. It's at camp where I meet more and more people who I can keep in touch with. If there's one thing I like, its meeting new people. I don't know why this is, exactly. It's probably because meeting new people means that they don't know I have bipolar and other mental illnesses. I don't know how harsh I'm being on myself. It's just how I view myself. I don't know any other way to view myself, unfortunately. I'm so deep in my misery that I don't dare view myself in other way. I know with my poor social skills it won't last long before the new people I meet will know that something is wrong with me. They won't be able to say exactly what, of course. They'll just know something is really out of place about how I act. At least I can try to act normal so that at first, they just see this girl Emma as a normal girl. After time this illusion will be shattered of course. I'm at one of the activities with a group of campers like me and two camp counselors. The title of the activity is called

Fear Factor – Legendary Lodge Style. One of the camp counselors explains the first round. We have to eat and drink the extra food that the campers didn't finish last week. The food looked gross mixed together even though it was new food. I passed the first round. The second round was a race and the third round was swimming to the water buoy. I didn't make the second or third round, sadly. I felt sad, but good at the same time after one of my favorite camp counselors explained that even though I didn't make it, I at least tried. After this activity I feel like I can go on a bit without worry. The next few days (Monday, Tuesday, and Wednesday) go by quickly because of the fun activities. I'm happy. It's Thursday when we climb the mountain. I hate the climb so much. It's worth it once I get to the top. We have Mass. I stand by the enormous white cross on the edge of the cliff when it's my turn to overlook the beautiful, stunning world. I look down at the lake below and the sky above. I love it. The thought of jumping off the cliff comes to my mind, but it goes from my mind even quicker. Yes, this bugs me, and I will think about it later, but for now I'm enjoying the pleasant and calm feeling that's overcoming me. I need to embrace this moment because once I leave Legendary Lodge, most of this will disappear. At least I can pocket this feeling until I really need it. That is if I can remember it. I let out a silent sigh as it's someone else's turn to look over. I walk away from the enormous white cross on the edge of the cliff. I walk away from the beautiful, stunning world. I walk away from this all. I don't regret walking away for one, and one reason only: even though I'm walking away I realize how blessed I am. No matter where I am, I am blessed. God may have given me pain. He may have given me struggle. He may have given me pressure. But God has also given me love. He has also given me bravery. He has also given me strength. The first three I believe he gave me is because he knows I can overcome anything my mental illness challenges me with. The last three I believe he gave me because they are tools to overcome anything my mental illness challenges me with. That's all I need. Friday comes sooner than I want. Soon it's time to say goodbye. Some cry. Some laugh. Some smile. Me? Well, I do all three. When I see Danny, I rush over to him. He hugs me, and I see his tattoo. It's the bible verse that says *I Shall Not Be Shaken.* I smile at this and I immediately know. There are going to be times when I can barely hold myself together and I just want to end my life, but I can do this. I can do this. I know I won't be shaken. I know it.

It doesn't make sense at all. I sigh and try to relax my muscles. I am so tense not to mention exhausted. I lay on my bed. It's so uncomfortable. It's so uncomfortable that it feels like bricks underneath me. I imagine myself taking the false bricks and building a prison around me in a way, so I can't let myself out. That way I would suffocate because the air wouldn't go in and out naturally. It would turn old and musty after seconds. All I do is get frustrated as to why I feel this way. I try and try and try to figure this out. It's only when I get up and walk to the mudroom and I see the calendar. I suck in a breath for quite some time before letting it out. I take my finger and trace past the numbers of the month of August in my mom's calendar on the wall. Past all the scheduled appointments, past some birthdays of my siblings' friends, past all the dates in August until I stop at the huge number 28. August 28th. August 28th. AUGUST 28TH. School starts on August 28th. My first year of high school. My freshman year of high school. I jump in the air and pump my fist. Yes. Yes. Yes. YES. I'm excited for once about school. Why? Well not for the reasons one should think. I'm excited because there are only four more years of freaking required school left. All if it. ALL OF IT. It'll all be done! Well this happiness only lasts for about a minute more before it all actually hits me. Four more years of hellish misery. That was the real reason why earlier I felt like I was in my own prison. I can't really say what has more of an effect on me. Is it being way more than halfway done with school or is it having to face the even more than halfway done with school? I don't know and honestly, I don't care because it's only the beginning of August.

The three "an"-words that I'm feeling right now: anger, anguish, and anxiety. Not a very good mixture. I'm walking down the halls of Helena High School with a red face. It's the second week of freshman year and I just got back to school from an appointment with Marie. She offered to introduce me to another person with bipolar. Ever since I could finally talk to her on my own without my parents I asked her almost every other second session if she found someone like me that I could meet. I never met a person with bipolar. I'm the only person I really know who has it. My Aunt Betsy did, but she killed herself by overdosing on pills before I was born. So finally, when Marie mentioned earlier today that there is a twenty-four-year-old my back stiffened, and I sat back.

"What?" My voice sounded startled and a million things were running through my head. My throat closed as Marie repeated herself. After I apologized about a hundred times and asked if she was mad the same number of times, I made my decision. That decision in the end was no. No, I wouldn't meet her. After the session now, I wonder if I made the wrong decision. My mind keeps going back and forth changing every moment. Yes, I made the wrong the decision. No, I made the right decision. Yes, I made the wrong decision. No, I made the right decision. All of this is driving me to the point of insanity even though I'm on my pills. What doesn't make sense is, if this is what I wanted all along, why am I saying no now? It doesn't make one bit of sense at all. When I reach my English class, I sit down in my desk wishing my mind would stop. It doesn't though, throughout the whole period. When the bell rings I walk out of class and wonder who I'm going to sit with for the whole lunch hour before my Earth Science class starts. I end up going to the library by myself yet again. I go to an open computer and start to write a random story. This clears my mind, and my mind slows down, thank God. I'm so distracted in my story that the anger, anguish, and anxiety disappear all at once.

I still run out of class a lot for the same reasons. I always go to my counselor because of this. She always comforts me. To help me, she let me drop one of my classes and instead I get to run passes in the counselor's office for one whole period. I like it a lot, except once I interrupted a class and saw people I know who treated me badly in the past. It's worth it though, because it's so much better. It's worth dropping a class. It doesn't matter what class, it's still always going to be worth it. That's how much I hate school. School is always going to be a struggle. I learned that in fifth freaking grade and possibly even earlier. That seems pretty young to me. I wouldn't be surprised if that's pretty young to most people. I don't realize that there's a possibility that this might be partly in my head. It might be all in my head. Who knows though? My counselor, Mrs. Avett, is one of the best people at my school. I go to her a lot with most of my problems. She helps me so much. During the period of pass running, I'm taking a break in Mrs. Avett's office. I usually do this when my mind is on a roll. The pressure is building, and I want to go home. I always want to go home. I call home a lot saying I'm sick, and even make myself believe that I am sick. I'm a hypochondriac for sure. During the morning I'm practically dragged out of my bed by one of my parents. While I'm taking a break, I tap my feet anxiously. I just want to go home. The bell rings a lot sooner than I wish and I grab my backpack and hitch it over one shoulder. I go to Health. I take my seat and count to five before looking ahead. We have a guest speaker today. She is a mother of twin girls who are my age. I used to know the twins well at church when we were only nine. I hardly remember any of it. It's almost surreal how I now block things from my past because it burns too much. The twins' mom, whose name I even forgot, has a huge smile. I don't get why she is smiling. The topic is rape, which I always get freaked out talking about. I get freaked out by talking about anything disturbing. I can't handle topics like that. It doesn't make much sense though, because I was never ever raped before. When the class is filled she introduces herself as Paulette. I'm a little bit shocked that hearing her name now doesn't even ring a bell in my head. I should have a light bulb go on in my head thinking, "Oh, I remember her." I don't, but it doesn't bother me much. Everyone's attention is on her as she begins to talk. They are all so intrigued that no one notices me squirming in my chair. The details she shares are gruesome. I sit in my seat as long as I can. After about a minute more I can't handle it. I take my backpack and hurry out of the classroom. I'm not even careful to avoid making a scene. I run to Mrs. Avett's office with tears running down my face. I'm shaking uncontrollably, and when I try to speak I end up coughing from my tears. I sit down on one of the chairs in her office and place my chin right on top of my shaking knees.

"Emma," Mrs. Avett says in her natural, soothing voice that always calms me down so much, and always makes it easy to tell her why I'm upset. "What's wrong?"

I hold my breath and then release it. I take a deep shuddering breath in and then start coughing on my sobs again. Mrs. Avett is patient, which is what I love about her among many other things.

When I calm down, I tell her everything. I trust Mrs. Avett so much that I say every detail I heard and how much it scared me. Mrs. Avett nods as she listens. When I'm done talking her hand reaches for the phone. I let out a panicked breath. She looks at me. "I'm just going to call your dad." Of course, Mrs. Avett knows what I need most. There was no need for letting out that panicked breath. She talks to my dad and takes the phone away from the ear to ask me if I need to go home. I say yes, at once. She talks to my dad some more and hangs up. "He was just as worried you wouldn't be able to make it through the day as I was," Mrs. Avett says. "I just asked you to make double sure that you wanted to." I smile glad that Mrs. Avett did ask. It makes me feel good. She is helping me by asking me the question as if I'm able to make my own decisions. I can make decisions in some ways, but Mrs. Avett makes me feel like I can make decisions in ALL ways.

Holidays are the worst for me. They always have been. Rewinding to a certain blast in the past at my grandma and Aunt Denice's. Just about everyone was around for Thanksgiving. What I mean by just about everyone means almost everyone on my dad's family side. My dad has seven siblings and all of them have more than one kid. That is excluding my Aunt Denice who has none, and most of us consider her a saint for many reasons, which makes her my idol. We were all sitting around the table eating the best Thanksgiving food that I thought couldn't get any better. Paul, my older cousin, had his girlfriend over. Of course, with my big mouth I kept asking intrusive questions. It was a question I asked at dinner when I figured out enough was enough. "Paul," I said between chewing huge amounts of food and looking at him. His eyes were filled with terror at what question I could ask which could be more humiliating than when do you plan on marrying Allie? Oddly enough I was oblivious to the terror in his eyes and asked the next question. "Have you been sleeping with Allie?" Everyone stopped eating and there wasn't even a sound of breathing. I looked around at everyone's shocked eyes. Paul's neck and face were so red that I knew at once that what I had asked was wrong. The first person to talk was my Aunt Ida who was going to pull me aside later on and tell me how inappropriate I was being, even though it wouldn't be her place to do so at all.

"Who needs some more ice for their water?" It made things more awkward in my opinion, the way most of my family forced yeses out of their throats in response. The rest of the night was horrible. The tension wouldn't stop growing. In fact, it grew at a pace that was unbelievable. Maybe it was just me, but I was almost sure at least half of my family felt it too. I looked down at my hands the whole night. After my Aunt Ida pulled me aside and told me how inappropriate I was, I felt shamed by her, and I knew I was going to get it worse at home. When I said goodbye, I quickly I ran out of the house and sat in the way back of the car. My parents, brothers and sisters followed. I took a deep breath in with tears in my eyes. No one else was saying a thing so I had to.

"I'm so sorry," I burst out. My siblings just looked out their window and my mom's hands were covering her head. I forced my eyes to look over at my dad. It was his family, so it was affecting him most. I could see it the way his muscles were strained in his neck.

"Dad?" I never knew when to stop.

"I'm so embarrassed," he said roughly. My mouth fell open. That was the last thing I would expect my dad to say. I had never heard him say those words. Those words coming out of his mouth were ones I never even imagined him saying. The fact that they could come out of his mouth never crossed my mind. When we reached home I got out of the car and ran into the house to my room. That night is one of the examples of my trying too hard because I feel uncomfortable on holidays whenever my family comes over. Another scenario is my not being able to handle holidays at all, so therefore I'm in my room all the time. That is usually what I do. Even if it isn't a holiday when my family visits, it's still hard not to escape to the deep depths of my bedroom where I can isolate. I don't know how I survive all of these events. It's a miracle, really. I hold my breath when I think about all of this. I can only imagine how this Thanksgiving dinner is going to go tonight. A lot of people are coming over. Not just my family, but my family's friends also. How could this get any worse? When the time comes around, I decide I'll try. It's better to try than not to try at all. I hope at least the saying is true. I start up the stairs only to turn back around and walk back down. I can't do this. I go to the darkness of my room and stay there until everyone leaves.

I'm staring out the classroom window. I don't understand what my teacher is talking about, so I tune him out. I breathe in as snowflakes form on the window. Snowflake after snowflake after snowflake. It's pretty, really. The snowflakes are too small to see the actual design they have in them. At first, I'm frustrated that I can't figure out the design. I squint my eyes to try to figure them out. It doesn't work. I open my eyes wide and try not to blink hoping I'm not missing anything. It's no use. I sigh and try to relax the tension in my muscles now. More snowflakes fall. They are smaller ones. The bell rings and everyone gathers their stuff. They rush out the door all excited for the weekend. I am too, but only because that means school is over for two days. I walk outside numb because I have nothing to do this weekend and numb because of the temperature outside. It has to be ten degrees below or colder. The snowflakes are still falling. I reach out to catch one. When I open my hand, it's gone. All of a sudden, I recall a similar memory. I was young. I was so young that I still believed in Santa Claus and the Easter Bunny and so on. I was laughing in delight. I was all by myself. The sun was shining through the slightly opened window in my parents' room. It was picking up the dust particles in the room. I was told before that they were dust fairies. I kept grabbing the dust particles and when I open my hand they were gone. I kept jumping up and trying to grab them in hope to see one. I wasn't disappointed in never catching one. In fact, I was happy. Now I'm trying to grab snowflakes. They disappear in my hand. I feel like crying. What's the point in being frustrated with not seeing a snowflake when you can just be happy that they're there in the first place? I keep trying to catch them. For once in my life I don't care what people are thinking of me. I don't give a damn if they're staring and snickering. I just want to be happy. Which I am.

I don't take my life year by year, week by week, or even day by day for that matter. I take it minute by minute, or more likely second by second. I never know when I'm going to break down and cry or lash out in anger. It sometimes happens so fast that I have no idea its coming. Yes, there are signs, but I still don't recognize them because of the speed they come or because I just refuse to. To me there's not much difference between them coming at the super quick pace and deftly refusing to acknowledge them. The signs come either way without much notice, so why should the speed matter. In the future I may catch the signs soon enough that I can dodge the breakdowns and the anger. Right now, though, I'm not able to. I'm getting to the point where school is just too much. I must try, though. I just must. I need to take my life slowly no matter what. Whether its minutes or seconds, I need to. I have to put one foot in front of the other. How do I know all of this? I know this because I'm having so many breakdowns and angry feelings. I can hold it in at school with only minor breakdowns and hardly any angry feelings, but when I get home it's a whole other story. When I get home, I let it all out. The uncontrollable sobbing and the loud screaming always gets the best of me then. I have been like this ever since I started school at age five. Put on a pretty smile while being tortured inside until school is over has always been the norm for me. My family knows this better than anyone. My worst fear at the moment is letting it all out at school, so therefore I must still try. I must, I must, I must, I must. I just must. I know all of this. I don't know everything though. I don't know how much everything will tear me down more and more. I don't know how much energy my life is going to drain from me. I don't know how much weight I'm going to drop which in result will make me look anorexic. I don't know how much sleep will leave me. I don't really know much about anything that's going to happen within the next few months. One thing that is for sure is that I'm scared. What will happen with that feeling? I don't think I want to know. For if I do know, then I'll realize that taking that minute by minute, that second by second is a waste. In the next few months I'll try something so tragic that it'll haunt me for the rest of my life.

I always read posts on Facebook that want you to "like" statuses and pictures. The pictures with words *like if you miss your childhood* are what catch my attention the most. There's usually 10,000 likes on it. I don't understand how people can love their childhoods so much. I know everyone's childhood is different. Like how some people say they were "carefree" and "without worry". I'm not quite jealous of the people who had good or rather great childhoods. Some part of me is actually happy for them. I still don't understand, though. I guess the reason why I don't understand is because I *can't* understand. I can't understand it no matter how hard I try. I'm betting this on one thing. I highly assume this is because I didn't have that "carefree" or "without worry" childhood. My childhood was far from all of this and anxiety and worries were around nonstop. From my parents always fearing what friend of theirs next I would call fat, to the abnormal bite marks on my hands, it was always very worrisome. The thing was, back then I didn't know the difference. I didn't know the difference at all. I'm guessing I didn't know the difference because I didn't have it any other way. I didn't realize that there even was a difference. So therefore, it never crossed my mind that I could have it different. I thought that was how it all went. Later on, learning that no one had to deal with what I had to deal with is painful. Of course, there were good times. There were amazing times even. They just aren't as clear as the hard times. That's probably the hardest part: not remembering what I should remember that made me feel happy. When I go on Facebook and see this I immediately scroll past it. It hurts my heart. Hopefully someday it won't affect me so much. Someday.

Silence is something I can't stand. It's a fact that can't seem to change. No matter what, nothing works. My mind is usually spinning a million times a second so there's no time for me to even consider taking a liking in silence. Just being in silence is something I can't stand. On the car ride from school after my dad gets off his cell phone, there is no noise at all. The country music was on right before my dad took his work call. I don't notice that the volume is all the way down, so I don't think about turning it back up. All I hear is silence.

"Dad," I say suddenly making him jump slightly. "Today at school I had a good day." He nods, and I keep on talking and talking with barely a breath in between. I'm talking so much that I don't even realize that I'm repeating things again and again. "Oh, and I had a really good day at school to—"

"Emma!" I look at my dad and frown. His muscles are strained in his neck. "Emma," he says again more calmly. "You don't need to repeat the things you say, and you need to breathe. Also, it's really okay to HAVE silence." I blink twice before responding.

"But I hate silence." It was something that I just realized now. My dad sighs and looks over at me.

"I know but silence is okay. It really is. You need to work on it. Do you do this with other people too?" I slink farther into the seat. I haven't really ever considered this.

"I don't think so," I say softly.

"Well you should work on it. People don't like it." I sigh in frustration.

"Like interrupting," I mutter under my breath. This causes my dad to laugh. "Emma, Emma. You sure can make people laugh though." I don't know what to say to this. I just smile. "Just try to work on it okay?"

"Fineeee." I look out my window just as my dad turns on the radio again. I feel smug at the moment because I realize that I escaped the silence.

As we continue to drive I write this fantasy.

Once upon a time there was a little girl who wished she was 'normal'. She asked to whoever was listening to her thoughts: Why can't I be normal? There was never an answer to her thoughts, so she gained the courage to speak up. She went to her dad and asked, "Daddy, why can't I be normal?" Her dad's face was stricken with sadness, but that sadness only lasted for a second because he didn't want his daughter to witness how much it pained him to see his daughter ask him this question. He forced a smile on his face and lifted the little girl in his laugh. "Oh honey. There is no such thing as normal." It relieved him to see the smile light up on his daughter face as she repeated his answer in a chant. "There is no such thing as normal! There is no such thing as normal!" The thing was, as time went on she kept asking and asking. The dad's answer was always the same: there is no such thing as normal. The dad was so troubled by his little girl's question that soon became daily thing.

"I want to be normal." I haven't asked this for a while. My dad turns to me. Tears blur my vision confirming my pain. "Everyone is normal, so I want to be normal too. I want to experience the normal everyone else gets to experience. I want to be normal dad. I want to so much." My dad puts down the knife he was using to chop tomatoes. I'm so focused on the wanting to be normal, that the thought of taking the knife to stab into my chest doesn't even occur to me. My dad answers me with a question.

"Is there such a thing as normal?" This question passes through me and I answer without putting too much thought in the question. Or rather I don't put any thought in the question and just answer with the pain I'm feeling as best as I can.

"It feels there is. I mean I want to be like everyone else. I'm exhausted. I'm so full of exhaustion. I just want it to all stop you know." I close my eyes, but the tears still slip out. This statement has a million others attached to it. It's full of I wants. What it's full of more is need. I need to be normal. I need to not disappear. I need to become someone, anyone, besides me. "I want" and "I need" seem like two different things. They meet up pretty easily for me though. I look up at my dad and see his stricken face of sadness. It doesn't change, which doesn't make much of a difference to me. Nothing seems to make much of a difference to me these days.

"I hurt." I don't wait for my dad's response. I turn to walk to my room when a surge of pain shoots through my head. I hold my head and let out a quick scream that doesn't seem to reach my ears because before I know it I'm sobbing uncontrollably. I'm letting out the storm that has been inside of me for the longest of time. I haven't been silent about my pain. I always tell my parents I hurt. I do tell them that as much as I can. They always do their best to comfort me. The pain is still always there brewing a storm inside of me no matter what I do though. Nothing I do or anyone else does works. The pain is too much. I stand up and stagger toward my dad who wraps his arms around me.

"Please Daddy," I plead. "Please, please make it stop! I hurt! I HURT SO MUCH!!!!" My dad hugs me tight.

"Emma, what can I do? What can I do to stop it?" He is almost as desperate as me. I'm not able see it through my tears of pain of course.

"I don't know," I whimper. "I just don't know." My sobs soon slow to a stop.

"Now why don't you get some sleep? It'll be different in the morning. Take your pills and sleep." I nod willingly, although I don't believe it'll be different in the morning at all. I'm exhausted to the point where I can't even feel anything now. The pain is still hovering deep down, I know that. All I want is to sleep. So, I take my pills without any thought and my dad tucks me into my bed like he did when in the past when I was a little girl. I fall asleep right away still feeling nothing.

My alarm wakes me at exactly 6:00. I roll to my side to shut off my alarm while letting out a small groan. School. I lay in bed for an extra thirty minutes until I actually do get up. I don't even sleep through the extra thirty minutes. It takes all of my effort to get out of bed and jump into the shower. When I'm in the shower I only put a little bit of shampoo in my hair. Conditioner isn't a must, so I don't think twice about it. I don't even bother using soap or body wash. I stay in the shower for less than eight minutes. The shampoo never comes out anyways no matter how hard I scrub or how long I stay in the shower. I take a towel but don't dry all the way. My hair is still wet, and I yank the brush through my hair to get through the tangles. I don't do it softly. I put my wet hair up in a ponytail. I don't put on any makeup. My acne is visible even though there is not a lot. I go eat a bowl of Mini Wheat's. When I'm done it's time to go. I don't brush my teeth. I don't even care to. I join Danny in the car. He is a night person. I can be either a morning or a night person. Today I'm a morning person. It's not a real good choice though because Danny is totally the opposite. It's unfortunate, really, because night people are usually cranky in the morning, whereas I am not. It's more unfortunate, really, because I don't stop at things even when night people are cranky. Today Danny is very focused on the road. I'm very antsy and want to talk. My dad's voice rings in my head and I repeat under my breath what he said last night when I complained to him that Danny wasn't nice in the mornings.

"Emma don't talk to him in the morning because he is very tired." I just want to talk whether it is to me or to Danny. Danny glances at me but turns his attention on the road as it was before. Hearing my own voice isn't enough. I turn to Danny and say what is commonly said in a normal conservation.

"How are you?" Danny sighs.

"I'm fine, Emma." He doesn't even look at me when he says that. This makes me even antsier.

"Aren't you going to ask me how I am?"

Danny sighs again. "How are you?"

"Good." He still doesn't look at me. Now it's my turn to sigh.

"Danny you—"

"Be quiet!" His voice is harsh, but I know he doesn't intend it to be. After all he's my big brother with one of the hugest hearts. This is probably why I don't stop.

"You could at least look at me you know!"

"I'm keeping my eyes on the road. It's icy and snowy so that's where my attention needs to be. Will you please stop, Emma?" Danny's voice has no hint of harshness. He's exhausted. I feel horrible now.

"I'm so—"

"Did you brush your teeth?" I frown and slink down in the passenger seat. This is all it takes now to really shut me up. So, I do.

There's two options when one is suicidal. The first option: to kill yourself. There's so much pain that one can't see through it. It's a thick fog that can't clear. It's a long maze that has no end. It's a black hole with no way out. Through the pain there is nothing but more and more and more pain. It doesn't seem to go away. There is no hope. The second option: to stay alive. Throughout all that pain there is strength. There is just enough strength to hold on. To grab onto the thinnest thread of what you thought was no hope. There it is though, the thread of hope. No matter how thin it is, it'll always be there. The hard part is that finding that thread of hope seems impossible when it's so dark. It makes it even more impossible to find it when suicidal thoughts cloud the brain. I'm at Marie's office clenching and unclenching my fists. I have been thinking of killing myself nonstop lately. I don't know why but then again, I never know why. It's a case that can never be solved. I stare blankly ahead not even realizing that there's a chair in front of me. I don't want to think about killing myself but there the thoughts are. They are never-ending. The door opens, and I turn my attention to it. It's not Marie but another therapist. She looks around the office and smiles when she sees me and shuts the door behind her. Her client isn't here. I take out my cell phone to see the time. It's 3:02. Marie is two minutes late. I clench and unclench my fists harder. I'm getting angry. I feel like taking my fists and pounding them as hard as I can into the wall behind me. Marie opens the door and I quickly let my fists loosen. I'm still angry, but not as much as sad. I walk to her office, not needing to follow her. I know the way by heart. I'm sure I can even find it with my eyes closed. I sit down on the all too familiar couch. Just as Marie sits down across from me I burst into tears. Marie sits patiently and quietly for me to finish. When I keep going she hands me a tissue. I shake my head not wanting to take it, but I do anyways. I wipe my eyes when I'm done crying and take a shuddering breath in.

"Marie. I don't feel like I can live anymore. My mental illness makes me hurt. I make me hurt. I don't know what to do anymore. It's too much. It's all too much!" I'm shaking. It's always been too much. I don't even know how it got to be too much. Marie folds her hands in front of her. I have a hard time looking her in the eye. I feel like somehow this is all my fault. It's obviously my mental illnesses' fault. If that's true, then why am I starting to believe it's my fault even more than my mental illnesses' fault?

"Emma." I force myself to look into Marie's eyes. Suddenly the atmosphere feels all tight and stuffy. I need to change that. I force a smile on my face. It's so unnatural in hurts but I ignore it. I stretch my arms out in front of me.

"Look how skinny I'm getting." Marie doesn't give the response I expect.

"You need to eat more." I let my arms drop. It's true. I do need to eat more. I have no appetite lately though.

"I know but I'm never hungry." I already lost ten pounds it feels like, but why keep track? Nothing matters anymore to me. Marie takes a piece of paper and pencil off her desk and hands it to me. I look from her to the paper to her again.

"What's this for," I ask uneasily.

"Your number. I want to have it, so I can call you each night to check in on you." This explanation makes sense. I nod halfheartedly. I take the pencil and write my number on the paper. I'm shaking while doing so. Marie takes the paper and pencil back and I breathe in deep. I don't do this because Marie expects me too usually. It happens naturally. The rest of the therapy session goes by without much talking. I'm pretty sure that's because I made the pain I was in clear enough.

I'm not eating. It's not that I don't want to eat. It's that I have no appetite. I'm not anorexic or bulimic. I can promise anyone that I'm not. When I force myself to eat, the food goes down my throat painfully and when it hits the pit of my stomach I feel worse. I don't have to join my family for dinner, at least. I want to join them of course, but I don't see the point. At least not right now. Besides I don't want to miss Marie's phone call. Last night she called to check on me and I felt better. I need my phone by me at all times it seems. I'm at my grandma's and aunt's house. They cooked dinner for us. They usually cooked for us on Wednesdays when I was younger. Once the Volesky kids grew older though it lessened and lessened. I honestly think this is better whether I have an appetite or not. Tonight, is one of the rare occasions that we eat at their house when no other relatives are visiting. Still I'm not eating. I'm glad I don't have to join them for dinner also. That is until I hear my dad's voice calling down the stairs for me to come eat. I ignore him at first but when his voice gets louder as he keeps calling, there's no use. I slam down the book I was reading and march up the stairs. My family is at the dinner table waiting for me. I see my grandma smiling at me and take a deep breath in. I try to let all my anger go. I sit down at the table. We all start to pray. When we're done praying we pass around the food to put on our plates. I take a little bite of mostly everything. I take a couple of bites of most of the food on my plate and I feel worse than worse. I'm all of a sudden really sad. When I'm sad I want to feel better. To feel better... I stand straight up and ask to be excused. I don't wait for a response. I run downstairs and run to my phone. I almost slip on the book I was reading when I grab it. I hold my breath praying that I didn't miss Marie's phone call. Sure, enough I missed it. I stiffen and listen to her voicemail. When it's over I put my phone down and grab my book. I suck in a breath and hold the book to my chest. How could I have missed the call? How could I miss it? Marie was the only person I could talk to about my deep thoughts, my deepest yearnings. Who do I talk to now? I swallow back tears and go to the guestroom. I'm holding the book to my chest still. I sit on the guest bed wanting nothing more than the pain to go away. I don't want to feel pain. I don't need to feel pain. I would rather feel nothing than pain. I don't know what do to. The pain is searing through me. I pull the book away from my chest and stare at it. The next thing I know is that I'm slamming it hard against my head. It's paperback but my force is strong. I choke back on the screams in my throat. I want to scream out loud, but I know better than to do so at my grandma's and aunt's house. After a full minute of slamming the book on my head I fall back on the bed. My head throbs to what seems to be the full extent of how much it can throb. I immediately regret doing this. Why must I do such things? I grab the book and leave the room. I don't look at the paperback book as I set it in one of the many bookshelves in the house because now I know it'll haunt me. Every object I hurt myself with haunts me. That's how it works.

I look up at the sun and shield my face with my hand. I spread open my fingers a little bit so some of the sun can shine through. It's enough to blind me still. Why must the sun do this with its light? Sunshine is supposed to make one feel good. It's supposed to make one feel happy. I head to change for gym. When I reach my locker, I blink repeatedly. The aftereffects of spots from the sun fill my vision. I probably look like a fool blinking like this but honestly at this point I don't give a damn about anything. I change, not thinking much of anything. I must look skinny but that doesn't even cross my mind. I hurt. I always hurt. I tie my sneakers and go join everyone in the gym. I don't have the energy to do anything and gym class doesn't help in the least. I'm somewhere else throughout gym. That somewhere is a type of nowhere. I'm here at the gym but then I'm not. When gym's over I go back down to the locker room to change. My ears perk up at what some girl is talking about.

"The test for Drivers Ed is after school next Thursday! I'm so stokedddd!" Another girl laughs excitedly.

"I know! I finally get to drive myself! It's so embarrassing when my older brother drives me everywhere."

"We don't get our license right away though ugh."

"Yeah it's a bummer but…." I tune out their voices as I get lost in my thoughts which lead to nerves. The first test is coming up. It's a test you have to pass to get to go practice driving with a teacher. I have been practicing driving around the neighborhood with my dad, but I gave him more than a couple of scares. When I'm done changing I head to my next class. I worry about the test throughout my next class. I manage through the rest of my classes without too much worry. When the bell rings I rush out of class to meet Danny in the parking lot. I go to his car and wait by the passenger's side door. When he comes out of class his girlfriend Jena follows. I smile and rush to hug her. She hugs me back. She is one of my favorite people. The smile I give her is a real one and hugging her is what I wanted. The thing is, I still hurt. This doesn't make sense. Everywhere I go, I hurt. I back away and wave goodbye. I get in the car. This doesn't make sense. I love Jena. I usually feel great when I see her. Why not now, then? Something is wrong. Something is seriously wrong.

The next few days I'm silent. In the past I used to express my pain through screaming and sobbing, through biting and pinching and cutting myself, through anger and rage. Now I'm just silent. The next few days are the weekend, so I'm at home. At school I pretend I'm happy. At home I don't pretend. I stay in my room most of time. I can't be around anyone. Anyone includes my family. I don't know why, because they know me. They know my mental illnesses. I just don't know why. At the moment I'm in too deep. Right now, it's all about death. I fantasize about death. It sounds so good. It seems so great. I want it. I want death. I want it so badly. I imagine going to the kitchen and grabbing a knife. I slowly get out of my bed and head for the door. The kitchen is just down from the hall. I could just grab a knife and get it over with. It would be so much easier with a gun but there is no gun in the house. I could overdose on my pills, but I can't do that because I swore to myself I wouldn't kill myself the same way my aunt did. I enter the kitchen and see Paul is trying to find something to eat. I swallow, and my head feels like it's going to burst. He smiles wide.

"Hi, Emma." His smile shows me he cares and he's happy I'm here. I know he is worried though. I can see it in Paul's eyes. I open my mouth to say something, but nothing comes out. Paul waits for me to reply. His smile stays in place. I can't think about how it will affect my family if I die. I'm in too deep for that. What I can think about is letting them know I love them. Maybe that way it'll change how I feel about death.

"I love you, Paul. Know that." I turn on my heel and walk away. I feel mania mixing in with the depression. I need to tell everyone I love them.

I barge into Megan's room. "I love you!"

I barge into Danny's room. "I love you."

I go Ellie. "I love you!"

I go to Jack. "I love you!"

I go to Nick. "I love you!"

I go to my parent's room. I hesitate and swallow. Tears brim my eyelids. I wipe them with the back of my hands and open their door.

"I love you mom and dad," I shout. It's not until after I shout that I see they're not in here. I run around the house looking for them. I'm about to freak out when I see them in the backyard. I run outside.

"Mom and dad! I love you!" My voice echoes in the sky.

"We love you too." I run back to the house. I go back to my bedroom and shut the door. I'm in too deep. I will kill myself. Just not yet.

I don't like how I feel. I hate how I feel. The end is coming nearer and nearer. The thing is I keep changing my mind in a way no one could ever understand. I will kill myself. I won't. I will kill myself. I won't. I will kill myself. I won't. It's on and off all the time. I guess one could say it's a way I hold off until I can't anymore. I'm so confused. I'm driving myself crazy. Or I would be, if I wasn't crazy already. There is one thing I know for sure: I want to kill myself. I just don't know what's holding me back. I tried dealing with it in so many ways. Now I will try a different way. One way that I never thought was possible. One way that scares not only me, but everyone else around me. Silence is done consuming me. I'm mad now. I'm very mad now. The pain is consuming me through madness now. I want everyone to know how I'm feeling because I need to. I'm done giving a damn. My hands are clenched into fists so tightly my knuckles are turning white. My teeth grind into each other so hard they hurt to an unbelievable extent. I breathe through nostrils so forcefully that I'm surprised I don't have a nosebleed. I swallow so hard that it's painful. I march out of the room, the torture within me growing and growing. I'm in the middle of the living room where half of my siblings are with my parents. I spit out the images I had earlier into high pitched words.

"I'M GOING TO KILL MYSELF BY STABBING MYSELF WITH A KNIFE OR BY BREAKING GLASS AND DO IT THAT WAY!" I march back into my room not wanting to witness everyone's faces at what I just did.

I want to stay home. But I go to school. Not because I want to go, but because I can't stand being in my house. It's hard. I go throughout the day like a zombie. The driver's education first test is today. I'm not even looking forward to that, but I know it's something I'll eventually want done. Besides I need to pass. It would be mortifying if Ellie, Paul, Jack, and even Nick drove before me. I'm not looking forward to driver's education anymore at all, but if it's what I have to do to get through the day, then so be it. I sit down at a table all nervous about the test. I sit alone. Before the test starts they show a short video about a drunk driver who killed an eighteen-year-old. I try to focus on it. When it's over some teacher talks about a lot of different things about driving. I zone in and out. When it's done the teacher passes out paper. She sets it in front of me. I stare the paper. It's not an actual test. It's to see what one knows. Easy stuff. I pick up a pen from the middle of the table. I start. Every question is one I don't know. I flip through the pages trying to find something I know. There isn't a thing. The teacher claps her hands.

"Times up!" Wait? It's timed? I look down at the paper. I didn't fill out a single thing. I didn't even guess on the multiple question part. The teacher comes to collect my paper. She doesn't glance at it, but my brain is already past the normal range of paranoia. I rush out into the parking lot. My parents are there with smiles on their faces.

"How was it?" I'm already in tears. I don't answer and hop in the back of the car. The back of the car. Will I always be riding in the back? I bury my face in my hands as my parents get in the car. They don't ask me questions. They are quiet. My mom drops off my dad at his work, so he can finish up some stuff.

"Bye Emma." I don't bother responding. I look up as the car turns off. I think my mom and I are at home, but we're at Safeway.

"Emma? Are you coming in?" I look out the window at the passing people in the parking lot and I can practically hear everyone whispering about me. Their eyes don't cross mine, but I can tell they are thinking and talking bad things about me. I clench my teeth. I want to yell at them to stop, but I have no courage, no energy.

"Mom I really want everyone at Safeway to STOP!" I say this half plea, half cry. My mom stares at me for a moment.

"Emma, what do you mean?" I stare at her for a moment now an incredulous look on my face.

"Mom! They're talking about ME!!! They are saying bad, bad, bad things that I DON'T like! I can tell it!!!!!" My mom nods.

"Okay I'll be quick." She doesn't understand. I pull my knees to my chest and put my hands over my ears and squeeze my eyes shut. I don't see them, but I can feel their presence. When this doesn't help I curl into a ball and sob.

It's Mother's Day and my family is out to dinner. It is a spring day, but the air is so hot it could be summer....

PART - 5

BACK AT INTRO:

On the ride home from the hospitalization I can tell a difference. It's been a week, a week in hell. It seemed more like an eternity in something more powerful than hell. Now, though? Now I can tell a difference in the world I have never seen before. The grass is greener, the sky is bluer, and the air is sweeter. I'm not quiet on the drive home. I talk and talk and talk. I'm a little nervous about seeing my siblings. It doesn't help when the thought of them hating me crosses my mind. Surprisingly, to me and my parents, I speak up about this. They reassure me how happy my siblings will be. Yes, I did see them once in the hospital. Or only some of them. They visited me, and I was nervous, but it turned out fine. I didn't see Megan or Danny at the hospital though. My older siblings I didn't see at all. My parents reassure me, and even more surprisingly I take their reassurance to heart. I believe them. I'm livelier than before. I can see that now, feel that now. When we enter Helena and reach closer to home my heart rate speeds up. I think about my appointment with Marie in two days. For some reason I'm a lot more worried about seeing her than anyone else. I don't know why this is. Maybe it's because I tell her almost everything about me. Things I can't tell anyone else. When I see my siblings I almost break down in tears. My siblings are holding signs that say Welcome Home. I run up the porch steps and hug them each equally and whisper to them how much I love them. I couldn't have made it without their love and support. My older siblings are happy. I can tell that the reassurance my parents kept giving me was a good thing. Ellie, Paul, Jack, and Nick are happy too. We talk, and we laugh. I haven't felt this way in forever and that's okay. It just means that I can treasure this feeling so much more. When it's dinner I go to the kitchen. I sit down and look eagerly at the food. For the past week all I have eaten is hospital food. Yeah, it was good but thinking about it now makes this food look so much better. As I take a bite, it tastes so much better too. The steak is cut nice and even. I take a fork and bite into its medium-rare juiciness. I bite into too much fat. I reach across the table and grab a knife to cut the fat off. And I don't think about how it could hurt me or others at all.

It stuns me that I don't have to go to school for the rest of the year. At first, it's just plain hard to believe. I'm happy and sad but mostly happy. I'm also stunned by my grades. All my teachers were nice enough to give me the grades I had before I left the hospital. Most of them were A's, a B, and a C. I smile a little bit. This is good. This is almost too good. I'm on the computer a lot. It keeps me busy even though I spend way too much time on it. One day after school Danny brings me cards.

"From some of your classmates," he says.

I look at them uneasily at first but then I take them eagerly. One is from my teachers. One is from my classmates. I read the cards thoroughly. They are all nice comments about telling me to get better. I smile wide. I see that Polly even sent me a card of her own. I'm shocked. She cares, but how much? Obviously, a lot. I don't know how to feel about this, and I realize that that's okay. Yes, I feel mad, sad, and happy at the same time. I can't forgive her. Not yet. I don't hold grudges. It's just something that's hard for me to forgive. Or is it just a matter of forgetting? I don't know. I'm just happy that everyone cares. It means so much to me. I put all the cards, including the ones from my family in the bottom drawer of my nightstand. I'll treasure these so much. I'm going to keep them forever. I let out a sigh. I know I'll still have to fight this illness at times, but at least I know life is beautiful. After all, if people can't let go of yesterday's ugliness how can they grab onto tomorrow's beauty? I lie down on my bed and stare at the ceiling. I close my eyes and imagine myself tomorrow and the next day and the next. I'm living for tomorrow's beauty and not yesterday's ugliness. And that is what living life is about.

The phone rings. I get frustrated when no one answers it. It's funny how no one likes answering the phone, especially in a household of nine. I run toward the phone. I answer it right before the voice message machine.

"Hello?"

"Are mom and dad home?" It's Megan. Her voice sounds clogged up as if she were crying. I'm usually misinterpreting things so I'm sure it's nothing.

"Yep." I head to my parents' room and knock. "Mom? Dad? Megan's on the phone!" My dad opens the door and I hand him the phone. I decide to go read. I'm a huge bookworm. I'm reading a trilogy and am on the second book. Whenever I don't understand a sentence I have to reread it over and over again until I can make sense of it. I can't skip it. I'm just starting a new chapter. I groan through clenched teeth. It's so annoying how I just can't skip it. I reread it for a full minute before I finally get it. Three chapters later I'm exhausted. I read a lot. It's true. One thing people mistake about me is that I'm not a fast reader. I'm slower than slow. I can thank the rereading for that. Ha! NOT! I go upstairs to take my pills and then go back downstairs to sleep. As I lay in my bed my head swirls with thoughts. They keep me up as usual. Eventually I drift off to sleep.

Megan comes home the next day. I look up from my book and greet her with a smile. "Hi, Meg!"

I go back to reading my book when she sits down on the couch next to me I look up again and realize she wants to tell me something. I put my book down.

"What's up?"

She smiles. "I have news to tell you." I nod. She takes a deep breath in. "You're going be an aunt." I blink once. I blink twice. Megan waits for a moment and then a huge smile crosses my face.

"Wow," I say. "That's awesome!"

Megan's smile grows. "Thanks, Em."

I pull her into a hug. It's surreal for sure, but probably not for long. That's how things are, I realize. Things are surreal, but in the end, it becomes as real as can be. Most things are like that. Other things aren't like pain. Pain is always real. It will always, always be real. Always, but so is familial love. Familial love is always real too. If you feel familial love, then you don't feel pain. If you feel pain, you don't feel familial love. It's all so real. As Megan embraces me back I think about this little baby inside of her. There may be a risk that she or he will have mental illness. A family who has mental illness in their genes means the risk is higher. No one knows for sure the actual cause of mental illness, but genetics is a huge factor. What if that does happen? I keep thinking about this as Megan gets up to probably tell my other siblings the great news. I try reading but somehow, it's too much. I click my tongue in frustration. Too much thinking makes me feel overwhelmed. I force myself to realize than I'm going to be an aunt, and a good aunt at that. Megan will be a great mother. I won't let her down. This baby will be blessed whether she or he will have mental illness or not. One thing is for sure: when this baby comes out into the world she or he will be loved unconditionally and eternally.

This baby may feel pain as she or he grows. What she or he will feel even more so is familial love. I will make sure of that, even though she or he will get enough love from the family without me. Yes, that's true but I am here. I am here, and I will love this baby like no other.

Summer is here. The highest it gets in Montana is about 100 degrees. I don't need to check the temperature to know it's getting up there. When I wake up my blankets stick to my skin and my hair is slick. I hold still, but the feeling is too much. It's too much that I don't only need to take a shower. I *want* to take a shower. I can't stand this feeling. I kick off my blankets and run to the bathroom. I take off my clothes and jump into the shower. The cold rush of water washes over me and I tense. It's cold but it feels so much better than being trapped in my sweat. Showering is a time to myself where I can relax and think. I let the tense muscles in my body go easily and I start to think about how far I've come. I've made it through fifteen years of hell of battling the cruelest of cruel mental illnesses. It almost took my life just months ago. Thinking about it makes it seem like it happened years ago and also makes it seem like it happened yesterday. It's funny how an incident can make it seem both ways. An incident that real and that powerful can do that. When I'm done showering I get out and change into my clothes. I don't go outside immediately. I go to my room and look at the cards everyone had sent me to feel better. I think about the forgiveness thing again. Not with just the past forgiving and the present forgiving. I think about future forgiving. Will I be able to forgive people so easily? It's such a big deal to me. Maybe it's just an obsession at the moment. Little do I know how much forgiving will affect me in the next seven years? Little do I know I will encounter a girl who is fifty times crueler than Polly and Gina? Who is so much worse, and that she manipulates me into doing things I don't want. Who makes me feel so bad that I'll slit my wrist with a razor? Little do I know I will encounter someone who I will meet through NAMI, fall head over heels in love with, and move to California for? Who will tell me he loves me, looks at wedding rings with me after asking my dad for my hand in marriage, only to break up with me at what I thought was our most precious spot under the stars. Who will tear me apart bit by bit until my heart bleeds, make me have suicidal thoughts, where I cry out loudly in pain. Who cut off all contact with me without a reason why? Little do I know that my mom will eventually have me see a clear vision on forgiveness: that someone can't force forgiveness, it'll come with time. I put the cards away after looking at them and shake my head as if to distract the whole forgiveness concept. I'm sweating again even though I just took a shower, so it's official how hot it is. Beads of it sweat threaten to go down my forehead. I go across my room to turn on the fan. When I do, the air the fan blows out pushes back the beads of sweat. I let out a light sigh and flop down on my bed. The whole forgiveness theory will have to go away for now and that's not because of my mental illness. It's because of me as a human. I need time. Just like my mom says, healing takes time and for once I'm okay with that.

I love stargazing. I always have, and I always will. I go stargazing as much as I can at night during the summer. I spread out a blanket and lay down on it, placing my hands under my head. I just stare, and I just admire. Mostly I wait and try to find a shooting star. I do see one at times too, but mostly I just look at the stars and get lost in them. There's something about the stars that will take my breath away. Their beauty alone is breathtaking. Even though they are trillions and trillions light years away they are so clear and bright. They die but they keep on shining. I hope to be that way someday. I want to leave a mark in the world to show that I survived mental illness. I don't know what is in store for me in my future, but it's got to be good, right? Something about tonight seems extra special. The stars seem brighter and my neck doesn't get as sore as it usually does beneath my head. I can stare at the stars longer without a blink. I see a shooting star and a smile crosses my face. Yes, I love shooting stars too. They flash across the sky and you absolutely can't blink. They're more exciting than the regular stars. Both types of stars mean the same to me though. I don't want to miss them. I think about stars some more and soon fatigue comes over me. I know I'll have to go inside. I'm drifting off to sleep when I hear my name being called. I sigh.

"Hold on! I'm coming!" I look up at the stars for one fuller minute. An unexpected thought crosses my mind. If there weren't stars there would only be darkness. Pure darkness. I stick my tongue out at this thought. It's good there are stars then. I don't know where I could be without them. I will make a mark in the world someday. I don't know how yet, but I will. That way I'll be a star in a universe. A star that signifies hope. After all, that's the thing I see when I stare at the stars.

Sophomore year approaches at a moderate and content pace. The break from my freshman school year and the summer was a good thing for me as well as my health. I needed it. Do I want to go back to school? That's debatable, but probably not. Do I need to go back to school? More than likely. Yes, my nerves are on high speed. I need to do this though. On the drive to school with Danny I'm quiet. Danny keeps glancing over at me to make sure I'm okay. This brings a small smile to my face. I would tell him I'm fine, but the attention is nice. This isn't fair to him. I tell myself that life isn't fair, but I'm not fully convinced. Guilt tugs, but the attention beats it. I'll have to feel bad later. Danny parks the car and I take a deep breath in. My hand shakes as I reach for the door handle. I know I have to do this. It's going to suck but there's no other choice but to go in. I open the door and get out of the car. The only reason I will try school without a fight is because I'm scheduled to go for only half days. My nerves are still on full speed. I shake a bit, but I remind myself that I'm fine. That I'm going to have to be fine. I mean, how bad could half days be? Well considering how I couldn't even get out of bed to go to school in the morning last year, it's obviously going to be at least somewhat bad. It's expected. High school is school after all. I force myself forward even though my feet are like lead blocks. It's going to be fine. I open the double doors to the school. I look around as if I'm starting school over. Well maybe I am to an extent. I'm starting a new chapter in my life whether it's school or not. I'm a brand-new Emma. Yes, I'm still fragile but I'm not as fragile as I was before the hospitalization. I'm trembling inside but I think I can do this. I enter the school and look around me. Everything's the same, yet everything's different. I go to the counselor's office to see Mrs. Avett. I hesitate outside the office and muster up all the courage I need to walk in. I don't know why I need courage. Mrs. Avett is Mrs. Avett. No school counselor can get better than her. I walk into the office where I see Wendy, who is in charge of keeping data in the computer and desk matters. She looks up at me and smiles. She has a granddaughter named Emma. Wendy has pictures of Emma. She looks like such a doll.

"Hi, Emma."

I smile back. "Hi."

I sit down in a waiting chair and look around the office. Different decorations are up, but the atmosphere is the same. I look at the wall mostly pretending to study the decorations when Mrs. Avett calls me. I go to her and she gives me a huge hug.

"How are you?" she asks excitedly. Her excitement is contagious.

"Better." Tears shine in Mrs. Avett eyes.

"Welcome back," she says and pulls me into another hug. I'm back at school with a new chapter. Hopefully this will be good.

I decide to try to go Homecoming this year. Last year wasn't successful because of my anxiety and paranoia. It's always a good thing to try again. I try to convince myself this, but I'm having a hard time believing it. The only difference this year is that Ellie is going too. She's going to go with her own group of friends and I'll just go and see who I can find. Megan helps me get ready. My niece has been in this world for four months now. She's is beautiful, and I love her to pieces. She's a new type of perfect. Megan let me borrow her beautiful sparkly black and gray dress. It fits me. I gained some pounds since the hospitalization, so I don't look anorexic anymore. Megan does my hair and makeup perfectly. When I look in the mirror I can hardly recognize myself. I let out a soft sigh at how beautiful the girl in the mirror is. I practice smiling. The smile comes naturally. This will work out. It has to work out. Last year at Homecoming I was really scared. The anxiety and paranoia were horrible due to the crowds of people. Oh God, the crowds of people petrified me! It was sad that I was petrified because these were people my age. Crowds always petrified me. I would think after 16 years I would be used to it. Nope. That's not the case. Last year anxiety and paranoia were so bad that I only stayed at the dance for twenty minutes at the most. I called my dad to pick me up right when he reached home and he would have to turn right around again to drive back to the school. This time I pray I can stay the whole time. If I think about it, I feel sorry for the past me. It's sad that I went through that, and that I might go through that again tonight. I pray again that I can stay the whole time. Ellie got ready with her friends, so I'll see her at the dance. I'll just say hi, and that's it. I love her, and I know she loves me. We just have different lives at school than at home. That's how it goes with siblings close in age and the same gender. It's something I have yet to fully accept though. Life may be better, but some things are just hard. I walk to the living room. I'm surprised at once. Ellie is there.

"Hi, El." She waves at me.

"I came back to take pictures with you," she says.

I nod in excitement. My parents take pictures of Ellie and me by ourselves and together. Paul comes up and Ellie and I kiss him on either cheek. I'm so happy to get a picture with Ellie and Paul and me because it hardly ever happens. When the pictures are all done, Ellie goes to meet her friends in their car and they drive off. I can't help but feel a spark of jealously. Not of Ellie, but what she has. I'm distracted luckily from this as my dad said it's time to go. I give Megan a thank you hug and kiss my niece on the top of the head.

"Thanks for everything, Meg." She nods.

"Have fun! Also remember to smile!" I have to stop myself from rolling my eyes. That's what my whole family tells me. They tell me multiple of times. I suppose I do need to smile more if they're saying that. "I love you, Emma."

"I love you too, Meg."

My mom stands by the door. "Honey, you look beautiful."

I give my mom a squeeze. "Thanks, mom!"

"Your dad's backing out the car. Now enjoy yourself and call if you need anything." I smile. I know anything means picking me up early if needed. I don't need to think about that right now. I go out the door with a light jacket on. I shiver. It's cold outside, but it's not winter quite yet. I put my cell phone in my jacket's pocket and head out to meet my dad in the car. I want the car ride to seem like it'll take longer than shorter because once we go out of the driveway my heartbeat begins to increase beyond its usual pace. The car ride goes by even faster than when I'm dropped off in the mornings for school. I want to tell my dad that I want to go back home but I can't bring my heart to do it. I don't want to disappoint him and my mom. Megan put in so much effort in making me pretty, so I don't want to disappoint her either. When my dad pulls in to the curb to drop me off I know there's no going back. I hold my breath and get out of the car.

"Thanks."

"Have fun and remember to smile. You're more stunning when you smile." I smile then because of the last sentence my dad said. I am more stunning when I smile. It makes me feel good. The smile or good feeling doesn't last long though, as my classmates scurry past me to get inside. I realize as I curl and uncurl my fingers how cold it is. I place my hand on my arm. It's very cold. I look behind me to see if my dad is still there, but he's already gone. My heartbeat increases as

I head forward to the school's double doors closest to the gym. I see a couple of girls from my English 2 class and some more girls who I'm more acquainted with. They say hi and smile at me. They cling to their date which makes me rigid. I never had a boyfriend before. Most of the girls here have dates and if they don't, they're here with friends. I'm alone. I decide right then that I can't let this get me down. I just can't. I at least need to try. I go through the doors feeling my anxiety and paranoia level up with my still increasing heartbeat. Once I'm inside I feel claustrophobic, even though I'm not on the dance floor. I turn to go when I see Mrs. Grayson. She is my math teacher who is supportive of me and always puts a smile on my face. Even better Mrs. Avett is right next to her. I walk briskly up to them. Hopefully I'll feel calmer around them.

"Hi."

They greet me with smiles. I hug each of them.

"Are you excited for the dance?" asks Mrs. Grayson. I hesitate but then nod. I am excited. It's not a lie. I'm just more anxious and paranoid than excited. Mrs. Grayson notices me hesitate but she doesn't say anything. I'm glad for that. She knows I don't want to be asked that in front of my classmates, especially when it's a dance and not a normal school day. Mrs. Avett smiles at my response. She doesn't say anything about me hesitating either. I head to the gym where the dance is going on. I know taking a deep breath in won't help so I just walk in. I'm overwhelmed at once. Everyone at the dance is in clusters. There are just so many clusters that are close together it looks like one big group that can't be separated. As more people trail in after me I have no doubt at once that within seconds it will be a group that can't be separated. I stay at the side. I want to go home. I'm so anxious. Oh, so very anxious. The paranoia isn't as bad, surprisingly, but it's there and I'm sure after a while it will grow. A boy heads toward me. I straighten my back. Someone is actually going to ask me to dance. I put on a smile that fades when the boy walks past me. I do my best not to look humiliated. Another boy heads toward me but he doesn't even spark my attention. It's only when he stops in front of me with a shy look. That's all it takes for me to know he's interested.

"Uh, want to dance?"

I nod eagerly. Hopefully the nod wasn't too eager. "Okay."

We go to the dance floor and start to dance. Well sort of. He is behind me and I'm in front. We swing our hips together. Grinding. It's what everyone else here is doing. It's really uncomfortable and I worry I'm doing it wrong. I guess I'm not because no one says anything. We dance, grind, or whatever for three songs. When it's over I say thank you. He nods and walks off. At once I wonder if saying thank you wasn't a good choice. I go to try and find some people I know. I say hi to a few and they respond little because they are too busy to care. I shouldn't take it to heart, so I don't. I head to the door, ready to leave. I call my dad and he said he'll start to drive over to pick me up. I wait by door for a few minutes until I feel a hand on my shoulder. Mrs. Avett looks down at me.

"Emma? Are you going home?"

I sigh. "Yeah I am. I can't handle crowds. Mrs. Avett. I don't think I ever will." Mrs. Avett shakes her head.

"Emma. Guess what? You stayed for an hour. That's forty more minutes than you stayed at the last dance you attended. I think that's a great accomplishment!"

I try to think back to how long I stayed last dance. It's all foggy. I believe Mrs. Avett wholeheartedly though. "Yeah. I guess that is an accomplishment."

Mrs. Avett is beaming. I don't know if this accomplishment deserves beaming, but I'll take it any day over disappointment. My dad pulls up and I tell him what Mrs. Avett said. He smiles and says he agrees. I nod and don't realize until I get home that I'm beaming too.

Sophomore year whizzes by quicker than I think. There are incidents that are unexpected. Like when I was in the back of Mrs. Avett's office. I saw a long knife that was used for cutting cake. Of course, I had an intrusive thought. I sucked in my breath and ran to get Mrs. Avett. She scurried to grab it and bring it to her office. I hovered by and kept biting my nails. She called me in, which I obeyed.

"Mrs. Avett?" I asked. "Did I do something wrong?" My voice was smaller than I meant it to be but how she scurried to get and bring it back with such an alert face on was surprising.

"Of course not, Emma! What you did was absolutely right!"

I nodded. "I was just worried that you wouldn't trust me if I showed you."

Mrs. Avett shook her head. "No, that's not the case. In fact, I trust you more. Thank you for showing me this. It shouldn't have been out there anyway."

The incident made me feel stronger and helped me gain more confidence. There were times when I'm constantly still bullied. Like with the three boys who stomped on my homework and threw my books everywhere in biology. I eventually had to tell the teacher because I couldn't handle it. I was also bullied in math class. The boy wouldn't stop so I told Mrs. Grayson, probably my favorite teacher who I ended up having until junior year that I would like to switch seats. I felt like a tattletale, but Mrs. Grayson assured me I did the right thing. And there were incidents when I joined a club where I felt like I could help others. Freshman year I met a girl who has the mildest form of Down Syndrome, but it was when I joined the club that we really connected, because that was when we realized how alike we were. We knew could never do things other people could do, let alone be "normal". It hurt a lot in a way, but more than that it was good too. It still is good with her. Sophomore year whizzes by quicker than I think but it also teaches me a lot of things about myself: I am strong, I am kind, I am compassionate, and I am beautiful.

PART - 6

I learned a lot sophomore year. It's junior year that is my turning point in my life though…. I am still strong. I am still kind. I am still compassionate. I am still beautiful. I am still a lot of things. I am learning I am things that I never thought I was before: courageous, reasonable, respectful, loving, and caring.

I learn these things because some of my teachers: Mrs. Avett, my past counselor, Mrs. Mure my current counselor, Mrs. Grayson my math teacher for my first three years, Mrs. Lewis, my JMG teacher this year. I learn these things because of my friends Stephie and Kait: my true friends in high school. I learn this because of Marie and Dr. Johnson, the best doctors I have ever had. I learn these things because of my family who are the ones who pulled me up through hell, even when I drug them down with me.

But what I am learning throughout all of this is what I am most of all: I am resilient. Whenever something, anything, pulls me down, I pull myself right up.

I try to think of this as I stand up in front of my U.S. History class to give my presentation. Everyone did a presentation based on the past. Mine? It's called: *Please Understand Me: Mental Illness*

Diagnosis and Treatment throughout the Past Six Decades. My mom stayed up working on it even after I went to bed. I have to thank her. She is the biggest blessing in my life for a lot of things. This is one of the biggest things she has done for me. She has done it perfectly. I have a paper to read from and there's a PowerPoint above me to give a visual. My teacher, Mr. McNalty, looks up at me. He nods for me to go and begins the timer. And so, I speak: "In 1988, just four years before I was born, my Aunt Betsy killed herself. She was treated for depression throughout her life. The problem was that my Aunt Betsy did not suffer from depression. She had bipolar . . . just like me." I look at my classmates as I speak my voice loud, so I can get the meaning across. I enunciate the important words. My face is serious. I keep talking about how, back in the 1950's, people with mental illnesses were often misunderstood and dismissed. It caused a stigma and the people suffered in silence. I try to get the point across of how serious it was and that even now it still has the same seriousness even if it's not as stigmatized. "I was diagnosed in the year 2000 when I was eight years old. My diagnosis was the result of looking at my symptoms, my family history, and tests such as a neurological tests and MRIs...." I keep going on about how it was different it was in the 1950s but for some reason I can't wait to get to the part about me. I keep switching back and forth and the slideshow helps my classmates understand, but I still like speaking about my life more. "I have mental illness. I have bipolar, schizoaffective, obsessive compulsive, and psychosis. But there is so much more to me than having mental illness." I go on and soon reach the medication part. "I have had many medications. Often, I have had to change medications due to side effects. I frequently have blood work done to monitor how the medications are affecting my body, especially my liver. If my liver has been adversely affected, I go off the particular medication. It is a delicate balance. Sometimes I have had to be hospitalized while the doctors tried to find the right "cocktail" of medication. The drugs I have been on have caused tremors, extreme lethargy, or mania. Those have been times I have had to try something different. In my case, because I was so young at the time of my diagnosis, I had to change medications and dosages often as I grew, and my weight changed. Some of the medications I have been on since I was eight years old have been Lithium, Risperdal, Seroquel, Abilify, Melatonin, Luvox, Lamictal, Vistral, Depakote, and Geodon. These medications control many of the symptoms of my disease. When I was first diagnosed, I saw and heard things that were not there, I washed my hands repeatedly, and said everything three times. I sometimes slept for days, and often stayed awake for seventy-two hours straight. I was either extremely hyper or so down that I was suicidal. The medications help to control some of my symptoms, but they do not all go away. They are just more manageable." I pause a second to let my classmates comprehend what I am saying. I look at the timer and see I have two minutes left. I talk some more and finally, finally reach the part I want to say the most: "It is a struggle, but it is something I take one day at a time. I know that someday I will go to college, marry if I choose, and will have children. I am not afraid to name my illness. I am who I am, and mental illness is a part of who I am." I say the ending and the timer beeps. I look evenly at my classmates with my chin held high. It's silent. Dead silent. And then a round of applause happens. They clap and clap and clap. It goes on. I smile and then I notice Mrs. Grayson there. My smile widens. After that I get a lot of compliments on how good I was, and how they could have never guessed I had mental illness. The latter shocks me, but I still smile. I gained a whole new respect from my classmates and that's something I will NEVER ever forget.

During senior year I meet the executive director of NAMI (National Alliance on Mental Illness) – MT. His name is Matt Kuntz. I am very nervous and shuffle my feet when I wait at Starbucks. He comes into Starbucks and we start to talk. I hand him my speech from junior year. He says he'll read it over and I tell him as much as I can about me. I'm honest about how sometimes it's still hard living with mental illness. It's always going to be hard. We talk some more, and I go home as he leaves with my speech. A couple of months later I get a call from Matt. He asked me to speak to the State Legislature about mental illness. I accept of course. The time comes, and I speak almost effortlessly. Afterwards I get a huge round of applause. By the end I'm crying and so is my dad. I'm actually making something of myself. I actually am. I speak at more places. It's when I am asked to speak for the NAMI – MT Walk that my heart nearly stops.

"W-what?" I look at Matt with incredulous eyes. He nods with a smile on his face. It takes a minute to sink in and when it does I jump up and repeatedly thank Matt. I go the NAMI Luncheon to speak days later. My sister Megan is there to hear me speak as well as my friend Kait, my grandma, Aunt Denice, and parents. Matt talks about the NAMI Walk and introduces me as their signature walker and speaker. I go up and begin to read my most favorite speech yet:

"Hi. My name is Emma Volesky. I am 18 years old and am here today to share with you how I experienced severe mental illness. This is my story:

All my life I have lived in fear of people thinking I was different because of my bipolar disorder. I lived in fear of others. I have also lived in fear of myself. I let my bipolar disorder define me. I couldn't name my mental illness or let it be a part of me. It was something I thought was out of my reach. I couldn't be in my own skin without the painful reminder that I would always have to deal with this pain.

I was diagnosed when I was eight years old, so I have dealt with the pain for years on end. Overtime I was also diagnosed with schizoaffective disorder with symptoms of psychosis and obsessive compulsive disorder. All of this added more pressure to the pain. It killed me in a lot of ways. There were struggles that caused me to isolate myself from the world and it made me believe that I was worthless.

At the time when I was eight I was suffering from hallucinations. These tormented me beyond belief. Sometimes it was stick figures moving around my bed and I couldn't breathe or look away until they disappeared. Other times it was visions of white creatures with deformed bodies moving back and forth between my room and the attic. They weren't dreams. I was awake, and they were as real to me as this paper that I'm reading from. There were times where I was so hyper I couldn't think clearly and stayed awake for 72 hours straight. There were times where I was so depressed that I couldn't stop cutting and slept for seventy-two hours straight. Yes, my mood swings were that bad. I didn't know how to deal at all. My mind went crazy during different situations.

The most horrid state that my mind was in was during my freshman year of high school. That year my life spiraled out of control. I was at the darkest of my times. I was put in the hospital for many reasons, mainly for the doctors trying to find the right "cocktail" of medication. There were more serious reasons though. Suicidal thoughts were nonstop, and I wasn't sane at all. It was beyond terrifying. I don't know if you can even imagine what that felt like. Sometimes, I swear that the suicidal thoughts are still dwelling deep inside of me.

Before I was in the hospital I was so paranoid that I couldn't even walk into stores without thinking everyone was talking about me. My parents practically had to force me out of the car for me to cooperate.

There were days where I didn't ever want to wake up and there were nights where I wanted to sleep forever. These seemed like the best options because I wouldn't have to think about the future at all. I feared the future so much. I didn't know if I could be successful or not. Nothing made sense.

Thankfully, I was able to get through that horrible time in my life. Slowly but surely after I entered my sophomore year I began to make some progress. Even though I couldn't fully realize that it was possible for me to become whoever I wanted to be, I was at least able to have some courage. I could go to school most days without running out of the class all the time. I then went to school half days which still was hard for me. I couldn't go to big events because my anxiety was so high when it involved noise and crowds. I wasn't social at all, so it was hard to approach my peers. I felt left out and there was no way of telling if people would accept me or not. I had trouble finding the right friends. It had been harder in the past, but it still hurt. I learned that not every single person is going to accept the fact that I have mental illness. There are people out there who won't accept anyone with mental illness. The only one thing that may be harder than that is that most times people with mental illness can't accept themselves at first.

I almost have accepted myself at this point. The thing that I have accepted is my mental illness. I realize that I have a really challenging brain condition, but it's nothing that I cannot overcome. I support

NAMI because it works to educate people who live with serious mental illnesses, their families, and the public about the realities of serious mental illnesses. They explain that mental illnesses are brain conditions, not different from any other biological conditions in the body.

Just like other medical conditions, treatment for mental illness can be very effective. I've been on over thirteen medications: Lithium, Abilify, Lamictal, Geodon, Risperdal, Melatonin, Remeron, Seroquel, Luvox, Depakote, Vistral, Saphris, and Latuda. I'm currently still on some of these medications. They make my brain at the most stable level it can be at. Often, I have had to change medications due to side effects. I frequently have blood work done to monitor how much the medications are affecting my body, especially my liver. If my liver has been adversely affected I go off that particular medication which makes it a delicate balance. The drugs I have been on caused tremors, extreme lethargy, and mania. Those have been times I have had to try something different. I was so young in my diagnosis, I had to change medications and dosages often as I grew, and my weight changed. My medication manages a lot of symptoms such as saying and doing everything three times or washing my hands repeatedly. Luckily, treatment made most of my symptoms goes away.

My treatment consists of my medication, weekly therapy, monthly visits to my psychiatrist for medication monitoring, blood tests, and self-care. For my self-care, I must take my medication when required, eating properly, exercising, drinking plenty of water, and regular sleep patterns. I can never drink alcohol or take illegal drugs because it could be fatal for me. While it's a lot of work, this medical treatment helps give me my life back. That's the same message that NAMI counsels all of its consumers and families. Proper treatment is a critical step towards recovery from serious mental illness.

Family support is also a key component of recovery. My family is the best thing that has ever happened to me. Without them and their support, I wouldn't be here today. That's something that I know is true 100% from my heart. Nothing can ever change that. NAMI works to help make families as supportive as possible to their loved ones that live with serious mental illness. NAMI's Family-to-Family class and its family support groups help keep our families on the same page as we go through this challenging journey together.

It's a long process, but recovery from mental illness is possible. I know that someday I'll go to college, get a job, marry and have a family if I choose. I'm not letting my mental illness define me and I'm not afraid to state my mental illness. I am who I am, and my mental illness is part of who I am.

Thank you all for listening to my story and for supporting NAMI. As Matt Kuntz has told me when he asked me to give this speech, "I'm living proof that the fight against mental illness is worth fighting.

Thank you."

It ends perfectly, and I realize that NAMI - MT has saved my life too.

I never thought I would get to this point in my life four years ago. Four years ago, I tried killing myself. I thought that it was the end for me. The hospital said it was suicidal ideation, but it was so strong, so real to me that I truly believe it was suicide attempt. All that pain.... It cannot be imagined how much it hurt. I still wonder how I am here today. What saved me the most? My family of course. Next? Being able to share my experience and how there is hope by speaking through NAMI - MT. And after that? The support of some other people too. I'm proud to say I was a reason too. I will be speaking next week, and I am excited. Yes, in the future I will suffer. I will go through hard times and suffer some more. That's what happens when one lives with severe mental illness. At least I now know that there is a light at the end of the tunnel even when it's too dark to see it through the thick fogginess of mental illness. I have been through hell and back. That's a miracle by itself.

It's Sunday. I'm at Memorial Park and I head for the podium. I step up to the microphone and lock my eyes with the 2,000 people waiting to hear with what I have to say. I smile. I'm here. I'm alive. I'm well. I have become the person I wanted to become but never thought I could get there. I open my mouth and then.... I speak.